Nine Days to Istanbul

The author in Vienna

Nine Days to Istanbul

by

Jeanne Frankel de Corrales

ONEWORLD

OXFORD

Nine Days to Istanbul

Oneworld Publications Ltd
(Sales and Editorial)
185 Banbury Road
Oxford OX2 7AR
England

Oneworld Publications Ltd
(U.S. Sales Office)
County Route 9
P.O. Box 357
Chatham
NY 12037, U.S.A.

© Jeanne de Corrales 1981, 1992

All rights reserved.
Copyright under Berne Convention
A CIP record for this book is available from the
British Library

ISBN 1-85168-037-3

Printed and bound in Great Britain by
The Guernsey Press Co. Ltd, Guernsey, Channel Islands

FOREWORD

SALZBURG. A many-faceted medieval jewel. Salzburg, the 'German Rome,' with its ancient Salzach River dividing its clustered domes, and its high hill topped by a fortress a thousand years old.

Here the trains were an important part of our daily life. Our city was a main stop on the way to Vienna, and many Bahá'í guests came through, so that those of us who pioneered here spent a good deal of time down at the railway station, watching and waiting for trains. There were endless steps to climb before you reached the tracks, and cold winds gusting when you finally arrived. It was quite a big place too. Once we actually missed a distinguished visitor who came to see us from Germany. Dr. Adelbert Mühlschlegel took a taxi that time, and we found him waiting for us at home.

In any case, our visits to the station were so frequent that a Persian friend once confided: "Marzieh, we have to go to that station so often, greeting people and seeing them off, that sometimes in the night I wake up waving."

As for the kind of trains that came through, if at this point you are thinking of Agatha Christie and the Orient Express: no.

Even so, the long trains kept some shreds of their their old magic. The travelers were beings set apart, in their warm, lit cubicles, wafting by above us - beings who had managed to take off from life while the rest of us only stood by and watched, dreaming about 'some day.' They retained a quality of enchantment, of the magician's cloak and wand – this even without that lonely whistle-shriek of fright and pain and loss that used to voice a train's true soul in the long ago, when it passed inexorably away from you into space and time.

We almost missed Jeanne the day she came to Salzburg, as she has said, but we managed a glimpse and a few words before she took off for Vienna and the East. I remember that she looked like Fifth Avenue, New York, in her high boots and cape, amid all the babushkas, drab overcoats, and bulging string bags. And luckily none of us could know that she was embarking on a train journey which would prove, in its way, as harrowing as anything a writer of mystery stories might devise.

Marzieh Gail
Keene, New Hampshire

NINE DAYS TO ISTANBUL

To my dearly loved mother
Margaret Bates

CHAPTER
1

IT WAS WARM INSIDE my first class coach. I leaned my head against the cold window gratefully. "Why must they put the heat so high?" I muttered to myself. Restlessly, I shifted in my seat and studied my fellow passengers. They seemed resigned to the discomfort. A bald, fat man across the aisle was coughing. The train was crowded. I tugged at the silk scarf around my neck: it was wet with perspiration. We'll all catch his cold, I thought grumpily.

The rapid express train moved across the white landscape of southern Germany. Soon we would reach Heidelberg and there I would change trains for Neckargemünd. The scenery softened from the stark industrial outskirts of Frankfurt to more gently rolling farmlands, now dreaming their winter sleep under a cozy white mantle of snow.

To distract myself, I opened my purse and pulled out the precious cable which had arrived a month ago —

just before Christmas – in Connecticut:

>   12 DECEMBER 1962
>   WELCOME PILGRIMAGE
>   WEEK OF FEBRUARY 3.

How long this news had been in coming! I had sent my request for permission to go on pilgrimage to Haifa in the Holy Land on December 12, 1955, the day after declaring my belief in the Bahá'í Faith in The Hague, Holland.

The Guardian of the Bahá'í Faith, Shoghi Effendi Rabbani, had been alive then, and I was bold, if not brash, to think that it would be possible for me to go immediately. Impatiently I had awaited his reply. When it came, it read:

>   REGRET POSTPONE PILGRIMAGE.
>   – SHOGHI.

How beautiful was that one word *regret*. I had clung to it through all the years of pioneering, of the formation of the first Bahá'í Local Spiritual Assembly of Nice, France, and the work of developing an Assembly at Orleans in the Loire Valley. It had been a beacon to us when the Guardian had sent Mother and me to the Nicobar Islands with the long months of waiting for the necessary government permissions at New Delhi, India. We had treasured that word during our time in Nicobar, and through the succeeding struggle with the Indian Government when they thought we were U.S. spies, forced us to leave our lovely islands in the Bay of Bengal, put us under house arrest in Madras, and confiscated our mail.

It was only now that we learned that the Guardian had cabled us in India during that troubled period, welcoming us to Haifa, all those years ago. How he must have wondered why we never replied to his cable. I ground my teeth in frustration: to have corresponded with him so often, to have loved him so, to have tried to serve and obey him, yet, never to have even met him. And he had died . . . died before the end of the Crusade . . . died before the election of the Universal House of Justice . . . died before we could meet.

My vision blurred with unwanted tears. My eyes, staring out the window of the train, saw nothing. I looked down at the cable on my lap. One big tear splashed onto it. I smoothed it out, then carefully folded it and replaced it in my purse.

In their correspondence following the cable, the Bahá'í international administrators, the Hands of the Faith in Haifa, had told us of the Guardian's invitation in 1957, and that they hoped it would be possible for us to make our pilgrimage to the Holy Shrines before the World Conference in London – this May of 1963 – which would celebrate the one-hundredth anniversary of the founding of the Bahá'í Faith through the Declaration of Bahá'u'lláh, its prophet-founder.

We could only afford to send one of us, and mother insisted that it should be me. She would stay in Connecticut and work to help me along the way. Certain economies were easy: such as the most reasonable air route from New York to Europe, via the non-jet Icelandic Airlines. Others were not. For a young woman traveling alone, the train still had to be first class.

We planned to break the long, exhausting hours of the transatlantic flight with a stopover at Reykjavik, Iceland. Then we allowed time on the continent for brief visits to Frankfurt to see the Bahá'í House of Worship of Europe, to Neckargemünd in southern Germany to visit Dr. Hermann Grossmann, a Hand of the Cause, at his home in the Neckar Valley. I would also visit Marzieh and Harold Gail in Salzburg, with whom mother and I had pioneered in France. Finally, I would stop at Vienna to obtain my visas for Bulgaria and Yugoslavia and participate in World Religion Day at the University of Vienna. It would be the first time the Catholic Church had permitted a priest to appear on the same lecture platform with other religions, thereby recognizing their existence. The National Spiritual Assembly of the Bahá'ís of Austria had requested me to represent the Bahá'í Faith on that platform. It was an exciting assignment.

From Vienna, the train across Eastern Europe would be the famous Orient Express. Then, from Istanbul, my journey would continue by boat across the Mediterranean to Haifa, arriving in the early morning. I imagined the golden dome of the Shrine of the Báb, one of the Bahá'í Faith's holiest places, nestled in the heart of

Mount Carmel, shining in the morning sun on the Bay of Haifa. What a wonderful way for a pilgrim to arrive!

The train began to slow and I collected myself. In the distance was picturesque Heidelberg – the city of universities.

I had to wait ten minutes at the Heidelberg station. It was cold: thirty degrees below zero, centigrade. The station master said that this was the coldest winter in thirty-three years. He was referring to the winter of '29. Although I missed Mother very much, at that moment I was glad that she had not come with me. Knowing how much she loved warm weather, I was sure she would have suffered on this journey.

I stood there, miserable in the freezing air, feeling cheated that I had been unable to reach the House of Worship near Frankfurt. I had arrived in high spirits only to find that the roads were completely impassable. Thinking that the next day might bring some hope, I had even risked the extravagance of staying overnight (though the extra cost for heat and hot water was too much for me in that expensive city, so I had to forego these luxuries). In the morning the roads were still closed, and I had to move on. Standing in the icy station, the morning's disappointment burned fresh in my memory.

The train finally came and I boarded. I arrived in Neckargemünd around 4:30 p.m. The conductor pointed across the street to a modern building and said that it was a hotel. I struggled with my bags (wishing I could learn to follow the Guardian's advice to travel with only one suitcase) and, after several halts to get my breath in the bitter cold, arrived at the door, which opened to the press of a button.

It turned out to be a factory for tapestries and lace instead of a hotel. But the sweet girls working there took me under their wing. They found me a taxi and a hotel and called the Grossmanns.

Really, I should have kept the taxi, but I was ignorant of the difficulties in obtaining it in the first place. At the hotel, I tried to hire another and found that impossible. The concierge of the hotel explained that I could easily take a bus. That appealed to me, so I set out.

Neckargemünd was a village right out of a storybook. More than a thousand years old, it has the narrowest cobbled streets in Europe, gabled houses, and half-timbered buildings — sometimes slightly askew and crooked — so picturesque you felt that all of a sudden time had been rolled back. Thin streams of smoke curled in the air from the many chimneys, and snow fell gently on my face.

I asked several people for the bus stop, but nobody seemed to understand me. Even worse, there was no agreement on the location of the Grossmanns' street. One lady said quite definitely that it was near the post office. Off I trudged through the snow, passing scenes from another age: the Neckar River frozen with barges piled on the ice dock; skaters bundled up, crossing the river, looking like a Currier and Ives print; an old man selling roast chestnuts over a charcoal burner. Fortunately, I found a small newspaper stand where they understood me, took me by the hand, and put me under the sign for *autobus* — a word I shall always remember.

The bus driver, in his turn, put me off at the Friedrich-Ebertstrasse. The number of the house was 39, and at the bus stop the number was 2. So one would think that number 39 was close by — no fear. One of the bus passengers went out of his way to accompany me, and we began the long climb of that snow-covered mountain. Soon I was panting, out of breath. I knew that the goal must be near, but up and up we went, at a very fast pace, in the now clear, icy night, with houses on both sides of the steep street almost buried in the snow. The street lights vied for supremacy with the stars.

When I thought I must surely expire, and my breathing had turned to painful, burning gasps, my kind guide left me at a gate facing yet another hill crowned by my goal. Steps were thoughtfully cut into the hillside for resting — and at last there were the waiting arms of Dr. and Mrs. Grossmann, who received me like a lost daughter.

These saintly souls took me in and warmed me in front of a great hearth with a blazing fire and gave me hot cups of some delicious beverage — I think it was camomile tea. Then they brought steaming, thick soup and homemade bread.

Mrs. Grossmann insisted that I take off my boots and from the corner of the room brought the most wonderful foot warmer. It was shaped like a huge, round loaf of bread, lined with fur and heated with metal hot water bottles. I slipped my feet into this ingenious device, which I was tempted to call a 'foot-muff,' and we sat at the table by the fire, talking on into the night.

Around the walls of the room were filing cabinets filled with materials on the development of the Bahá'í Faith in Europe, particularly in Germany. And then more on the doctor's travels in South America.

The doctor told me that he had first heard of the Bahá'í Faith in Leipzig from Harlan Ober, who had just been to 'Akká on a visit to 'Abdu'l-Bahá, Bahá'u'lláh's son. The Master had said to him, "Now, go to Leipzig and speak on the Faith at the Theosophical Society." Mr. Ober had done so, and that night Dr. Grossmann attended the meeting and accepted the Faith. It was 1920.

Dr. Grossmann became the first to visit Shoghi Effendi in Haifa after the Guardian's marriage to Rúhíyyíh Khánum. He was elevated to the rank of Hand of the Cause in the first contingent appointed by the Guardian in 1951, and was among the last pilgrims to be in Haifa before the beloved Guardian's passing in 1957.

In their great love and kindness, the Grossmanns would not allow me to venture out into the dark night again – snow had begun to fall once more. They phoned the hotel to tell the manager that I would be staying with them on the mountain. And there I stayed, remembering a day in Holland (at the dedication of the Bahá'í Center in The Hague) when the doctor had explained the effect that spiritual individuals can have on their environment. He had said that the footsteps of the followers of God change the very stones of the buildings they inhabit into new stones, the brick into new brick, the wood into new wood. I knew that the radiance surrounding this storybook home came from the saintliness of its inhabitants, and the warmth filling my heart came from the heat of their love – reflected from that of the Guardian – for all the friends: indeed, for all mankind.

The next day, Dr. Grossmann accompanied me to the station, even helping with my bags, and put me on the train for München. When the train pulled away, and I could no longer see his loving face or even his farewell wave, I was amazed to find that my tears had frozen on my face. So cold was it that drifts of ice had grown inside the train compartment: the heating pipes were completely frozen. Still the warmth of the love of Dr. and Mrs. Grossmann kept me warm for the long, slow hours through the frozen countryside of southern Germany – through the Black Forest, passing iced lakes and towering, sugar-cone mountains with ice-crystal trees. This was surely to be the perfect pilgrimage.

CHAPTER
2

MY TRAIN ARRIVED IN MÜNCHEN. The huge station was foggy with steam rising from the engines. I stood up, wrapped myself in my long black cape, settled the fur-lined hood on my head, smoothed my black leather gloves, gathered my luggage, and opened the window as we slowed to a crawl.

Porters scrambled to take the bags from passengers who handed them out the windows. The porter who had won the battle for my bag started to run when he heard that I was going on to Salzburg; the train from Frankfurt had been late.

He was not young, but he was strong. We ran the long platform (first class always seems to be at the rear of the train) around the front end of the locomotive, where kiosks displayed magazines, thick pretzels, coffee, Brötwurst, beer, souvenirs — everything. Crowds milled everywhere, and we could hardly get through them. I was puffing; the porter was not. He grinned at me with a toothless smile. "Goot, goot, Fräulein. No vorry, vee make it."

The train, smaller than the express, was on the last track (naturally), and it was steaming. We ran down the platform and a conductor called to us to get into a nearby second-class car. We wouldn't make the first class. "It doesn't matter. Hurry!" I told him. He tossed my bags into the open door and pushed me up the stairs. We were already moving. I grappled with my purse, pulled some Deutsche Marks from the zipper compartment (too many, I later discovered), and collapsed into the nearest seat.

Salzburg was beautiful with its spires against the snow. So medieval, with its winding streets, cobbled and narrow; its fascinating shops, and the smell of hot bread in the freezing air. It was dusk when we pulled into the station.

I had written to Marzieh and Harold, but only just, and it was possible they hadn't received my letter. Now, with the sun down, it was cold. My breath froze in the icy air. The hotel was in front of the station, perfect for my early-morning departure for Vienna. This would have to be a short visit.

Salzburg is justly famous for its many elegant old-world hotels, one of which was built from an ancient castle. My hotel was not one of these. It was small, modern, and economical. The tall glass doors were hard to open against the wind. This was not exactly my idea of quaint Salzburg, but it was clean and neat, with all the comforts. Best of all, it was convenient.

I hadn't realized how tired I was until I threw off my outer clothing, collapsed on the bed, and reached for the phone on the nightstand.

Marzieh's number was in the book. I dialed, still somewhat out of breath from my dash from the station, my hurried climb up the stairs, and the anticipation of seeing these dear old friends who were some of my favorite people. Marzieh was all the romance, the beauty, and the mystery of the East, and Harold was the logic, the calm, the pragmatism of the West – the head and the heart. Marzieh, with a Persian father and American mother, who, as a child, had stood at the knee of 'Abdu'l-Bahá, was now a lecturer and writer of history. Harold was her steady, constant support and protector. He always reminded me of a Knight of Old with his Lady Fair. They were a wonderful couple.

We had served together on the Bahá'í Local Spiritual Assembly of Nice, France. Harold had been the treasurer and his quiet, thoughtful approach to life's problems had been very evident. The Assembly had been served by Persians, Americans, and French – with every word translated into three languages. Marzieh, as chairman and interpreter, had conducted the meetings with a never-failing patience which was an example to us all.

Their phone rang. Once, twice, three times – no answer. It's early yet, I thought, maybe they're out. I would try again later. I put the receiver on the hook and lay back on the bed. Just a few minutes rest . . .

Two hours later (quite dark now), I awakened with a start. "Good grief! What time is it?" I called down to the desk.

"8:15 p.m."

"Is the dining room still open?"

"Yes, Fräulein, until 9:00 p.m." There was still time for a quick bath. I dialed Marzieh and Harold again. An unfamiliar voice answered in German.

"Is Marzieh there?" (Would he understand me?)

In halting English, he replied, "No. Both avay at zee Vinter School in München."

My heart sank. "When will they be back?"

"Late tonight, I belief."

"Will you take a message, please?"

"Natürlich."

"Tell them that Jeanne Frankel is here at the Hotel Europa, and that I have to leave for Vienna at seven in the morning. And I am so eager to see them."

"Ja, Fräulein, I tell zem."

What a disappointment! It would be a pity to come so close and miss seeing them. I hung up the phone and wearily drew water into the oversized tub in the bathroom.

There is nothing more wonderful in the world than the baths of Germany, Austria, and Switzerland. There, people truly understand the curative powers of a deep, foaming, luxurious, steamy bath. The hotels always have small packets of bath oil ready to put under the fiercely running water. Soft bubbles came up to my neck. I lay back, relaxed, and floated to the top of the water. Heaven! The ache in my bones from the long hours on the train slowly drained away from me. I moved my toes lazily as steam rose around me.

Now, this was the life. I almost fell asleep again, but my empty tummy kept me awake. Reluctantly, I pulled myself out of the lovely water. A large, warm towel was ready to my hand. It went around me almost twice (another luxury of bath-conscious people). I dried hurriedly, slipped into fresh underclothes, dug out my gray wool skirt, pulled on a gray cashmere sweater, pushed the brush through my hair, ran the lipstick quickly over my lips, and glanced in the mirror. Not bad. Thirty-two years and still quite a young girl looked back at me: no lines, skin rosy from the hot water. Not fat (oh, she would never be as thin as she wanted to be, but not fat, definitely not fat). She would do. I ran out and down the stairs to the dining room, never dreaming that it would be a long time before I would be able to enjoy the luxury of my own private bath again.

At six the next morning the phone rang shrilly. How could it be time to get up already? I had slept snugly under my soft, goose-down comforter. The dinner had been good and filling – if lonely, the dining room almost empty, and the service sleepy and resigned.

Everything was ready for the bellboy when the phone rang again. It was Marzieh! They were hurrying to the station for a short reunion before the train pulled out. Hurray! Of course – everything would work out. How silly I was to have worried!

It was a gray-white morning. People scurried to their jobs with their heads down against the brutal wind and their bodies bent against the cold. My boots crunched on the snow. Whew! It was much colder this morning. I stood beside the train stamping my feet and blowing into my gloves to warm my fingers. Where were Marzieh and Harold?

Five minutes before the train was due to leave, I caught sight of them running toward me, waving their arms in the air: Marzieh, her almost-black hair curling in ringlets around her face, her cheeks flushed from the cold, and her eyes sparkling with merriment; and Harold, his blond head hatless and a long muffler not quite covering his broad smile. Warm embraces. Tear-filled kisses. We climbed aboard to get out of the wind. We had only a few minutes. We looked at each other – so much to say, no time to say it. My memory was filled with the long evenings we had pored over the maps of the Ten-Year World Crusade. There had been so few virgin posts left open when I had become a Bahá'í that winter of 1955. We had wanted to go to Spitzbergen, in the far north, together. Well, maybe we hadn't made it to Spitzbergen, but at least two of us had made it to Nicobar and the Cocos-Keeling Islands –

Mother and I. We all missed her that morning. Now, I was on my way to Haifa. We said little, held hands until the whistle blew, and cried as the train left them waving on the platform and carried me farther east to Vienna. It would be years before we saw each other again.

CHAPTER
3

THE WHEELS BEAT A HYPNOTIC tattoo on the rails. I rocked with the movement of the train across the long stretch to Vienna. There were frequent stops. The landscape looked bleak. The sky was a dark gray-white. The compartment was either too hot or too cold – something was wrong with the heater.

Luncheon was dreary, greasy, and lonely. My mind turned to the coming lecture that afternoon at the university. Normally, I don't like to prepare my material, counting instead on inspiration from the audience. But this was a memorable occasion. The university was imposing and formal.

The dining car attendant brought his little cash box to the table for payment. We settled up and I wandered back to my car. The train had slowed to a crawl. There seemed to be very few people on this trip. But it was a Sunday – or maybe the weather had kept them from traveling. Time passed slowly. It seemed that we were hardly moving. I began to worry: would we be on time? I stopped the conductor. He pulled out his large vest watch, untangled the chain and frowned: "We are running more than one hour late, already."

"Oh, no."

He shrugged. "It's the snow. There's been an accident on the line."

Now I really began to worry. It would be terrible if we didn't get there in time for the meeting, I fumed to myself. So many were counting on me. Every time the train stopped, I chewed my nails . . . and prayed. It began to snow, lightly at first then harder, the farther east we went.

Interminable hours later, the outlines of Vienna showed dimly through the snowy mists. I was ready, standing with my bags by the door, when the train slowly – oh, so slowly – pulled into the station. The minute the steps were down, I was off. I grabbed the first porter and began to run. I needed a taxi, badly.

Fortunately, there was one right at the entrance to the station. The driver was sympathetic. Though the windshield wipers pushed the snow aside, there was almost no visibility as we raced directly to the university. No time now for a hotel, a change, or a warm bath. That would have to wait. It was already after four. What would they think? Minutes later (that seemed like hours), we pulled up in front of the massive doors.

"Where is the lecture being held? Which hall?" I left my bags with the watchman at the door and raced down the long gray stone corridor. It was freezing – there was no heating – but I was perspiring. The auditorium was filled. The audience (more than seven hundred in attendance) had kept their coats on.

I walked unceremoniously onto the stage. The Catholic priest was speaking. My long black cape flying around me made me look like a witch, something out of another era. My boots clumped on the wooden floor. The speaker frowned. There was one empty chair on the platform with a program on the seat. The Buddhist priest, next to me, smiled thinly. We were to speak in the order of the appearance of our Prophets. What luck! My turn would come last. As quietly as possible, I caught my breath. In spite of the cold, I felt clammy and hot.

Slowly, the stage stopped spinning and the audience came into focus. It was my job to sum up the past, explain the present, and pray for the future. Of course, there was no way to know what the first speakers had said, but, as I calmed down and listened, I felt confident – not of myself, but of my material. Everything would be fine: Bahá'u'lláh had written it all. All that was needed was to stick to His script.

To this day I cannot remember the exact words I used, but when it was all over the audience gave us a standing ovation. I called on my fellow speakers to share in the tribute. My stiffness and tiredness were gone.

The Viennese Bahá'ís crowded around me. They were all smiling and pleased. All of a sudden I remembered that I still had no hotel and had eaten nothing the whole day. It was almost 8:00 p.m.

We retrieved my bags. One of the friends said, "We must rush. The hotels close down around the university by 8:30. You won't get in if we don't hurry!"

Fortunately, there was a vacancy in a hotel directly across from the campus, but the place was uninviting and dark. The dining room was closed. I begged the headwaiter to find me something – even a cold sandwich. He shook his head. The kitchen was closed, and that was that. "But surely there must be something?" I asked.

"Maybe some hot chocolate," he admitted sullenly.

Moments later, large plates of whipped cream were placed in the middle of the long table. The Bahá'ís stayed to chat. We drank hot chocolate – many cups – I don't know how many, but probably much, much too much.

When, reluctantly, the friends got up to leave, we had finished the whipped cream. I dragged myself up the stairs. My first view of my room was not inspiring. The toilet was down the hall; the bathroom, the other way. They had turned off the hot water at eight. I was too tired to care. The tiny narrow bed felt lumpy, but nothing could have kept me awake.

Around two o'clock the next morning, I awakened feeling feverish. I tried to lift my head from the pillow.

I rose up on my elbows but suddenly fell back, so dizzy I couldn't see. The room whirled and I must have passed out, for when I came to, the bed was drenched with perspiration.

Again, I tried to sit up, but nausea swept over me. Somehow I must get to the toilet, I thought. With great effort, I swung my legs to the floor, felt for my slippers, and stood up shakily. Thank heavens I had slept in my robe! I staggered to the door, unlatched it, and peered down the dark, narrow hall. There was a tiny light burning in front of the W.C. It looked so far away.

Slowly, holding onto the wall, I tiptoed down the bare wooden corridor. With every step the boards creaked. I mustn't awaken the other guests, I thought. How can they not hear me? In the quiet hall, each creak sounded like a rifle shot. Finally – it seemed like ages later – I reached the door. There was a tiny cubicle, barely large enough to turn around. Absurdly I thought, what would happen if the door sticks? I was sick.

Back in my room, sweating with relief, I picked up the telephone. I must get a doctor . . . when have I ever been this ill? The room still whirled. I couldn't stand up or even sit straight. Oh, where was the operator? I clicked the bell: no answer. Oh, no, the switchboard must be closed! What should I do?

After more than an hour and innumerable trips to that horrible cubicle, my face was streaked with tears of frustration, nerves, and illness. I sat exhausted on the edge of my bed – weakened and chastened. What was it? The chocolate and whipped cream, of course. "Oh, Bahá'u'lláh," I cried aloud, "there is no one to help me. I am all alone. Please, please help me. I am too ill to pray."

Then a strange and wonderful thing happened. It sounds impossible, I was still so nauseated, so weakened, so hopeless of human help. But I sat there, hardly holding myself erect, when suddenly I felt a Hand on my shoulder – it was a Hand of love and care and tenderness.

I lifted my head and smiled. The Hand seemed to stroke my head. An indescribable feeling of comfort and warmth filled me. Immediately, I felt completely well. "Thank you, Bahá'u'lláh!" I called out. "Thank you." I turned out the light, but the room was filled with brightness. Sleepiness overwhelmed me. I was safe. I was protected. I slept.

Vienna was beautiful with the sun out. The Bahá'ís came over to spend the day with me before the train left that afternoon for Budapest and Belgrade.

The sky was cloudless. In the parks and on top of St. Stephen's Cathedral, the snow was shadowed with blue. Pigeons pecked at crumbs in the sidewalk cafes on the Kärntnerstrasse. It was cold and crisp. Gorgeous porcelains tempted me from the shop windows.

After obtaining my transit visas for Bulgaria and Yugoslavia, we went to hear the beautiful Vienna Boys choir. Sitting there, I was filled again with the wonder of the miracle that had saved me. Bahá'ís believe that a miracle is only a miracle for those who witness it but there was no doubt in my mind about what had happened to me only hours earlier. Here I was, strong and well, and feeling perfect. The young voices soared, with my heart, in praise of God and His works.

At four in the afternoon, they took me to the station and put me into my sleeping car. They had brought a white plastic shopping basket which they gave to me, filled with oranges, cold meats, a warm loaf of Viennese bread, and chocolate. But, even in the hard days ahead, I would *not* eat the chocolate.

CHAPTER

4

THE ORIENT EXPRESS! Its very name evoked a thrill of mystery. For almost one hundred years it had been host to the famous, the celebrated, and the notorious. Kings, emperors, and Oriental potentates had graced its corridors. Courtesans, secret agents, and spies had manoeuvered inside this moving caravanserai. How many treaties and world-affecting deals had been negotiated here, while the wheels turned! It was the most famous train ever to run, and it had been directly responsible for opening the land route between Paris and the countries of Western Europe through the Transylvanian Alps to the Balkans and Istanbul. Over that land route had moved the products of the industrialized countries in one direction, and the oil barons with their fat contracts and concessions in the other. They were followed by the soldiers of the two World Wars, and finally the refugees of the destruction caused by man's greed and bigotry.

The train left exactly on time. The brightness of the day had faded into the familiar gray-white that presaged another storm. When the train pulled out, it was already snowing.

My compartment was quite comfortable – a long way from the original teak and inlaid marquetry of the original cars, but the mahogany walls were polished and shining. The draperies were not made of flowered damask, but the heavy blind would guarantee privacy. The deep armchairs were gone, and in their place was a long sofa covered in some rather dismal blue-gray cloth textured with a fanned feather pattern, rather rough to the touch and with pillowed armrests for lounging. Across from the sofa were double connecting doors – now closed and locked – to the next compartment. In the corner was a cabinet containing a washbasin that pulled down from the wall under a mirror and some shelves. I unpacked the few things I would need for the night. When I was finished, the conductor stored my cases away and informed me that dinner would be served in about an hour. My traveling book was interesting, but thoughts of the train and the romantic trip ahead of me kept me from concentrating.

The history of this Orient Express was intricately woven into the tapestry of the tempestuous story of Europe. Yet now the airplane, which covered the distances so quickly, was taking its place. The Simplon Orient Express, extinct now for almost a year, had been one of the last vestiges of the grace and service of another era. It had covered the distance from Paris via the Simplon Tunnel in Switzerland through Venice and Trieste, and then split at Belgrade, one section going on to Athens and the other to Istanbul. Now all that was left was the Direct Orient Express. I felt a sadness for those 'other days.' Stories had it that the Simplon even had a bath car. Wistfully, I remembered that there had not been any hot water earlier that morning in Vienna. The little basin would have to do. I sighed.

The train moved slowly through the gathering twilight. Through the misted window I could see that the snow was deep. Snowdrifts almost completely buried some of the houses we passed. This was clearly one of the worst winters Europe had seen in a long time. Arctic winds swept down across the steppes of Eastern Europe bringing below-zero temperatures and blizzards. It will be dark when we reach Budapest, I thought. Oh well.

It seemed no time before the headwaiter passed along the corridor with his tinkling miniature xylophone, announcing: *"Le dîner est servi. Premier dîner."* The first sitting: the restaurant car was open.

I made my way past the other compartments. My car was almost empty, and so was the restaurant car. It was easy to see why they would drop this section at Belgrade, where we would join the main body of the train from Paris.

Dinner was unhurried and delicious: a fillet of sole with a bottle of Perrier water, followed by some kind of fruit pudding. A rather sad yellow rose shared my table with me.

The conductor had made my bed down during dinner. He came along to see if there was anything I wished to order for the night and to take my passport so that I wouldn't be disturbed when we crossed the border into Hungary. Our car would be sealed while we passed through this country.

I undressed and slipped between the crisp sheets and turned on the lamp at the head of the bed to read. Te *ta*, te *ta*, te *ta*, the rhythm of the wheels lulled me to sleep long before we reached Budapest.

CHAPTER
5

SILENCE AWAKENED ME. The train was silent. No wheels were turning, no gentle movement. We had stopped. I peeked out the window. It was still dark, very dark. The window was frosted with ice. My watch read nine o'clock. Good heavens! It must have stopped. No, it was still running. Then it must be morning; but it's still dark. My thoughts were confused. I rang the bell for the attendant. No answer. I sat up, yawned, and rang the bell again. Soon his steps sounded along the quiet corridor. He knocked on the door. "Come in," I called.

He slid the door open. *"Oui, Mademoiselle?"*

"Where are we?"

"Near Belgrade, Mademoiselle."

"How long before we arrive?"

"About two hours, Mademoiselle. Would you like a cup of coffee?"

"Very much, thank you. And a sweet roll, please."
"*Trés bien, Mademoiselle.*"

The compartment felt chilly. I got up, washed my face, brushed my teeth, and slipped on my warmest clothing, including a big woolly sweater. A knock came on the door.

"Your coffee, Mademoiselle."

"Come in," I said, pulling the door open. He put the tray on the table by the window.

"Shall I make up your bed?"

"Thank you." I stepped into the narrow corridor, sipping the coffee. The attendant quickly folded the bed into the wall, revealing the backrest of the sofa. It all took less than a minute.

"I'll change this after we retire this section at Belgrade, Mademoiselle. You relax now." He pulled up the blind.

"What time is it?" I asked, uncertain because of the darkness.

"Eight in the morning, Mademoiselle." Somehow I had gained an hour.

"Why is it so dark?"

"It's snowing quite heavily, Mademoiselle. The train is delayed."

"Oh."

Another bell rang, down the corridor. He hurried away.

The coffee was hot, sweet, and very black. The plate of rolls held a fat croissant, some Viennese pastries, and a small pot of jam. They were delicious. Well, this isn't too bad, I thought. I've had a good sleep, and I've never been to Yugoslavia. It'll be fun to see the countryside. I tried to rub a circle in the frosted window. Outside, it was pitch black. I couldn't even see the snow falling.

Sometime later, my eyes growing sleepy again, I looked at my watch: ten o'clock. Had I reset it before? I couldn't remember. I put down the book, opened the door, and stuck my head out into the corridor. A few people were wandering up and down, but they spoke in hushed voices. The train remained quiet. It was still quite dark but I could see the snow falling. It seemed to be coming down hard. Had two hours really passed? Suddenly, the train gave a lurch. Good! We were finally going to move on. But no, it stopped again. Resignedly, I returned to my compartment and began to fret. Would we arrive in time? Would the main train wait for us? The conductor had said two hours. He was an optimist. The delay was no longer a game.

I was too bored to read. I dug out my writing materials to write to Mother; she would love the story about Vienna. I wrote long sheets of close script. More time passed. Finally I put the letter away. A grayness had filled the sky, but it still wasn't possible to see much. Snow battered the window. Pulling open the door, I looked out. The conductor was at his seat, at the end of the car.

I wandered down to him. "What is happening?" I asked. He looked at me dully.

"We are still stuck in the snow, Mademoiselle."

"Yes, I know that. But what I mean is, when will we be unstuck?"

"I don't know, Mademoiselle," he shrugged.

"But we'll miss our connection at Belgrade."

"Maybe not."

"Can we find out?"

"No, Mademoiselle. The lines are down."

"What are we going to do?"

"Wait. Just wait, Mademoiselle. There is nothing else to do. The plows will be here soon."

Back in my compartment, I slipped into my cape to see if I could get off the train for a minute. The corridor was empty. I pulled open the massive door between the cars. It was supposed to be automatic — hah! A blast of cold air went right through my cape. The outside doors were locked. The train was still sealed. There was a sudden jerk. We started to move. Slowly at first, with more jolts and stops, but we were moving. I hurried back to my compartment.

Lunchtime came and went. No headwaiter came by with his musical bells. They had only put on sufficient supplies to reach Belgrade, and that time had come and gone hours ago. The dining salon just offered coffee and drinks. I turned to my white plastic basket. Those dear friends had thought of everything. I made myself a thick sandwich of salami and bread. There was no knife, so I used my nail file to cut the long loaf. Was it my imagination, or was it getting colder? I rang for the conductor.

"Is there any way to make it a bit warmer?" I asked when he finally arrived. He looked tired.

"No, Mademoiselle. I'm sorry. The pipes have frozen."

"Is there any news about when we shall arrive? It's getting so late." I shivered in the cold air from the open door

"Soon, Mademoiselle, soon." Quietly, he shut the door.

I fretted: it did no good. At least we were moving. Finally, I must have slept. The train jolted to a stop and I awakened to peer out the window. By the street lights, each with a dim halo, a few deserted avenues could be seen. An occasional figure moved ghostlike through the darkness. We passed some uninspiring buildings, dark and abandoned. Where are we? I thought. This *must* be Belgrade! As if on cue, the train pulled into the station.

CHAPTER 6

WITH A TERRIFIC SCREECH the wheels ground to a halt. The conductor knocked on the door to take my luggage. He had a strange look and avoided my eyes. "What's the matter?" I asked.

"The connection from Paris left some time ago," he admitted.

"Oh, no! What am I going to do now?"

"There is another train on the next platform ready to depart, Mademoiselle. There are no sleeping cars, but there are first-class coaches. It will go fast and catch your train."

There was nothing else to do. The attendant helped me onto the platform. I slipped some paper money into his hand.

The train, pressed into service from the Yugoslavian State Railways, was sitting directly across the tracks, with its black engine steaming and ready to attack the storm. There were no porters to help with the bags. I struggled and slipped through the milling crowds of stern-faced, bundled up people who were pushing roughly to the doors of the cars. Inside was warmth and shelter from the freezing wind that howled through the vaulted roof of the station, bringing eddies of snow and sleet. I spotted a large number 1 on the side of one of the coaches. The steps were steep, so I tossed my bags up and pulled myself up after them. The first compartment was empty. It seemed plush enough, with deep, red velvet seats and curtains with gold tassels. There was nothing for it but to take off my wet boots and step on the delicate cushion to put my bags on the rack overhead. A draft of cold air came in from around the edge of the window, so I chose an inside seat near the ashtray on the wall.

I had no sooner sat down, with my cape still on, when the door to the compartment opened and an immense woman filled the entrance. She was dressed all in black, smiling a toothy grin and muttering to me in a language I couldn't understand as she pushed her way into the compartment, followed by three others. Inwardly I groaned. They were evidently one family. There was a slender, young girl of about twenty, also dressed in black but with a hint of a white blouse beneath her thin coat; a tall, stringy, young man – probably somewhat younger – his straight hair cut short over the ears and standing absolutely straight up on his head, and a young boy of around seven or eight who had thick, curly hair and huge eyes. He was dressed in some indeterminate, dingy gray and his skin was pale, almost transparent like parchment. They chattered quite happily in their strange tongue, getting settled. I thought of looking for another compartment, but the corridor was crowded now: impossible to get out. I grimaced as the old lady sat down – no, not sat, plumped down at the window. Her heavy bosom heaved. I smiled at her tentatively. "Do you speak English?" I asked.

She looked blank. *"Nein, Fräulein,"* she answered in German. *"Sprechen Sie Deutsch?"*

"Nein," I said sorrowfully, and watched them organize a picnic from their big overflowing basket. The grandmother worked efficiently with her rough, square, strong hands. Her face was round and gentle, with few lines but tired eyes. Her head was bare, and her hair, streaked with gray, was dark, cut shoulder length but unstyled. Even in her strange tongue, she clucked like a mother hen to her children and grandson. She laughed often. Her hands fascinated me. They were hands that scrubbed floors, and if she found time to knit, it was with thick wool and large needles. These were not hands that worked petit point or crocheted lacy doilies, but they were strong hands. She had a good face and kind; it was hard to imagine her with violence or cruelty. She had probably never been to a beauty salon.

The picnic made me realize that I was starving. Out came a thick piece of salami, crusty bread, and a bottle of something yellow. What could that be? The young man took a knife, sliced off a piece of the meat, and handed it to me with an inquiring smile. I took it gratefully, and he handed me the bottle. That I took more gingerly, pulling out the cork, smelling and taking a tiny sip. A fiery liquid poured down my throat. "*Was ist?*" I gasped. They all laughed.

"*Arak. Gut?*"

I handed it back, still choking. "*Gut* . . . but *nein, danke.*" I knew so little German. What could that other language be that they spoke? "*Was sprechen Sie?*" I persisted.

"Bulgar," the grandmother said with pride.

Of course; they were Bulgarians. We were heading next into that strange land, now a Communist state. My interest intensified. I opened my basket and contributed oranges and some of the chocolate. They were pleased and looked at me with approval. My throat still burned from their *arak*.

"*Woher kommen Sie?*" the young man asked me.

"The United States."

"America?"

"*Ja.*"

"Oh!" They studied me as if I were an alien from another planet. Their eyes were curious and wistful. Here we were, strangers from opposing countries, forbidden by lack of diplomatic relations between our lands to be together. Yet, here we were. There is no way to bottle up people any more. Somehow, even without a common language, we were going to get to know each other, and in our doing that, a crack would appear in the iron curtain. People getting to know people: that is the way to destroy barriers. We were all smiling, letting our smiles replace the words of good will that our tongues had yet to learn.

The train gave a sudden lurch. We were finally on our way on the second lap. But we were so late — or rather, the time tables had ceased to exist. I wondered how this train could ever catch up with the Orient Express from Paris. The train picked up speed out of the city. I dozed.

When I awakened, it was colder. There was no heat at all. I struggled up from the mass of humanity surrounding me to go to the bathroom. The hall was colder still. When I reached the W.C., the pipes were frozen and only the extreme cold kept it from having a ghastly odor — ugh! I hurried back feeling dirty, grubby, and desperately in need of a bath.

The night dragged on. The train crept ahead, slowly twisting through the mountains. It was a pity we could see nothing. The storm raged outside the carriage. Finally, even the draft from the windows was blocked by the ice forming around the edge. I shivered and wondered if this was the area of Count Dracula and his famous castle. It well could be from the sound of the wind and the swirls of snow. I dozed fitfully, awakening from time to time. My compartment-mates were talking. I wished I could understand them: something seemed to be bothering them. The young man, Ivan, sat in front of his mother, whose name was Stara. His eyes darted quickly at every noise: a thinly concealed fear came and went from those eyes like a light turned on and off. They sat with their heads close together. Ivan's hands, which seemed too large for his body, dangled from long thin arms. His feet, too, were large and rather inclined to clumsiness. He seemed to be an obedient boy, kind and yet somewhat shy. Undoubtedly, he was good with animals – a boy from a farm, a boy who would soon be in the army, a boy on whom life acted, but who would not act upon life. What was he saying now? They all seemed so innocent, but somehow worried.

I looked at Anna, Ivan's sister. Her eyes were large, round, and dark, with a sadness in their depths as she watched her mother. Her hair was long and straight and pulled back from a center part. She held it by an elastic band – not a pony tail, but just to keep it out of her eyes. She spoke seldom. When she did, her voice was soft and apologetic, as if she were afraid to break into the conversation of others – or even the silence. She, too, seemed an obedient child – more capable in the kitchen than outside – a help to her mother and with her young nephew. I wondered what had happened to his mother, Anna's sister.

Early, (it must have been around five the next morning) the sound of their voices grew louder. I stirred in my sleep, and they hushed. But something about their talk puzzled and disturbed me. Not their words, of course: they were unintelligible to me. No, it was their tone of voice. They were frightened.

I sat up, stretching from my cramped position. The grandmother looked at me with questioning eyes. I felt – knew – that she wanted badly to speak to me.

"*Ja, meine Frau?*" I began.

She tried . . . slowly . . . each word . . . but I couldn't get it. Finally, she gestured to Ivan. He took down one of their cases, checked to be sure the curtains were drawn, and stationed Anna in front of the door to guard it. I became more and more intrigued.

They wedged the case into the seat, opened it, and carefully extracted a large, beautiful, ivory and painted crucifix. They handed it to me. I looked at it admiringly. It was obviously old – very old – heavy, of solid ivory, painstakingly carved and painted. The antique paint had chipped off here and there. It had a beautiful luster in the dim light of the carriage. "It's lovely!" I exclaimed.

She seemed to understand and nodded her head. *"Es ist von meine Papa."*

She pulled out her Bulgarian passport. Slowly I began to understand. They were afraid to take the crucifix across the border. They wanted me to take it across for them. I looked into their faces. I couldn't refuse. They were violating the law of their land, but it was a law against God and man. I slipped the cross under my cape. Stara began to laugh, then tears filled her eyes and she gave me a big hug.

That was settled, and none too soon. Ivan had given his mother a long swig from the yellow liquid – I had firmly declined – when the train grated to a stop.

We could hear the door of the coach open and the heavy boots of the customs and immigration officials. I didn't worry too much, with my U.S. passport. They had only given me a transit visa, but a U.S. passport was strong medicine in 1963. My new friends were solemn. Stara's children were quiet, their eyes wide open and unblinking.

The policeman opened the door. He, too, was not smiling. Icy air came into the compartment with the officials who followed the policeman. They left the door open, careless of our comfort.

Not one word did they say to me, although their eyes were hostile. Probably they couldn't speak or even read English. Conscious of the heavy cross under my cape, I didn't want to antagonize them, so I kept quiet. The customs officer ignored me, but dumped everything from the Bulgarian family's luggage all over the compartment. My heart was in my throat for fear he would strip us all down. But no, he closed the door on the mess he had left behind. We all looked at each other and grinned. We did it! Whoopee! I helped them pick all their things off the seats and floor and placed the cross lovingly in the largest case: their few pitiful clothes didn't take up much space.

After the excitement of the border crossing, things became more grueling. We were all so cold. We were all hungry. I went up and down the train, looking for a dining car. Nothing.

Outside, the storm raged on. Daylight came. There was no coffee, no milk for the children. There was no water. The pipes were frozen and heat was only a memory. The day was not as black as the day before, but dark gray. The landscape was as forbidding, as inhospitable, and as bleak as my mood. Then suddenly there was a crash! The train came to a very sudden stop. I was thrown from my feet on top of Ivan. What had happened?

Ivan went out of the compartment and down the corridor to find some answers. Avalanche! The engine was burried in snow.

We stomped up and down the hall to keep our blood circulating. With the train stopped, everything seemed to freeze. We must find a warmer car, I thought. Again I went through the train, forward and then back. Nothing.

There were many more people now, filling the coaches, all huddled together against the cold. And sometime during the night another section of the Orient Express had joined us, attached onto the rear of our train. It was hard to say exactly how many people were now marooned with us in the mountains of Bulgaria. Instead of our catching my train from Paris, another one had caught us. What a situation, I thought with disgust. Oh God, what time *was* it?

Now my watch had really stopped. The hours seemed to blend into each other. The daylight was short lived. We talked as much as possible to distract ourselves from our hunger. We talked with few words and many gestures. Bit by bit, I learned that they had been to visit family in Belgrade who had given them the money to travel in comparative comfort. I learned that it was a measure of the hardness of their lives in Bulgaria that although Stara and her children were some of the 'lucky ones' with outside contacts, the specter of fear and sadness never left them.

This hardship would be constantly reflected in the faces of the crowds that lined the tracks of the primitive railroad stops across this grim countryside. Crowds who said nothing, did nothing, but stared with blank eyes – sometimes hate-filled eyes – at the fortunate passengers on the train that carried them to freedom. We, the passengers, were trespassers on the land of the bleak and drear.

Before we knew it, darkness and night had returned. The train did not move. There had been no lunch and no dinner to follow no breakfast. The baskets in our carriage were pulled out again. We had tried to be frugal, but there was very little left. Some crumbs of hard bread and the end of the salami were scraped together. I had one orange left. Better save it, I thought. The children will need it in the morning. I was so thirsty and sleepy, but Stara wouldn't let me sleep. She kept rubbing my arms. I must sleep, I thought. Stara kept rubbing my hands.

When I awakened, she was still rubbing. First she would rub the little boy, then she would rub me. Ivan and Anna took turns rubbing each other. How cold could it be? I wondered. Much less than zero. Finally, the wind died and the storm abated, for a moment at least. The sun tried to come out. I looked outside. The snow came almost up to the window. Dear God, we are buried in it!

With daylight, the two engines were freed and the one from the rear pushed while the one in the front pulled. A dangerous task, but it worked. With a loud tearing noise, the train pulled free from the imprisoning snow. We all cheered. Our enthusiasm was dampened only by our extreme hunger. I couldn't even feel my fingers. Ivan offered me a drink of the *arak*. This time I took it.

As long as the train moved, we were happy. When the train stopped, we were silent, afraid.

It must have been around four that afternoon when the train finally pulled into Sofia. "We shall be all right now," I told Stara in English. Somehow she understood and nodded. But the doors remained shut. They were frozen.

Even though it was bitter outside, we opened the window of our car. It was wonderful to see civilization again. But the faces that stared back at us sent another chill into my heart. Astonishingly, they all looked alike.

Their eyes stared at us with that familiar dead expression. No life, no hope, they were like zombies or robots. They looked at my mink-framed hood belligerently. Our breath froze in the air and dropped heavily to the ground. We closed the window.

Despite this depressing reception, I felt excited. Surely they would have a dining car here. I called the conductor as he passed. "When do we eat?"

"You don't," he grunted. "There is no food for the train."

"No food?" I wailed. "But there are hundreds of hungry people on board!"

"No food. This is Sofia. Everything is rationed."

"I must get off and call the Embassy," I cried.

He shrugged. "Try it, if you want, but don't miss the train." He pulled the door open.

I jumped down on the snowy platform. My feet had almost no feeling, bringing me to my knees on the icy cement. Nobody came to help me up. Painfully, I pulled myself to my feet and stumbled into the station. There was a telephone on the counter. I reached for it and dialed zero. Even here, '0' meant 'Help!' "Give me the American Embassy," I begged, praying that the operator would understand me.

"No American Embassy." The dial tone returned.

I dialed '0' again. "Give me the American Consulate."

"American Mission?" she asked.

"American anything!"

The phone rang. "Hello?"

I almost wept with relief to hear an American voice. "We badly need help! We are on the Orient Express for Istanbul" (forgetting, for the moment, that this was not strictly true).

On the other end, in the background, I could hear a man's voice saying, "We don't want to get involved with that train."

"I heard that," I said loudly into the phone. "What do you mean, you don't want to get involved with our train? I'm an American citizen and I need help."

"I'm sorry." The phone clicked and the dial tone returned again. I slammed the receiver back onto the hook.

Exasperated, I realized that I must seek help away from my own country. Why does this seem so often to be true? I picked up the receiver again and dialed '0'. "Give me the British Embassy, please."

"No British Embassy. Do you want French Embassy?"

"Yes, please. The French Embassy . . . anything."

A sweet feminine voice with beautiful Parisian French answered. She didn't speak English. My French would have to do. Telling her the story, in French, somehow I was also listening to it. It sounded so sad. Tears rolled down my cheeks and froze into crystals of ice.

The French Embassy people were sympathetic. They would come right down to the station and bring some hot soup. I wept my thanks.

Now we were afraid that the train would leave before they arrived. But soon (sooner than I could have believed), there they came, carrying soup in a huge caldron – the kind that used to hang over the open fireplaces. The passengers crowded around. There wasn't enough to go around, but the children all had some. It smelled so good. A sharp pain went through my stomach and my head felt light. Still, maybe it was just as well that there wasn't enough.

They say you stop feeling hunger after awhile. I'm not sure that is true. Never once did I stop feeling hungry. Yet, we were all so grateful to the French that day. We felt that someone at least knew and cared about us. We weren't totally abandoned. We all cheered and waved to those kind diplomatic personnel; for all we knew they had saved some lives.

After the train had left Sofia behind, I began to realize that soon my friends would arrive at their destination. It was already late. How many days had it been since I left Vienna? I had lost track of time. We were all still hungry and cold and without rest. Darkness came quickly.

Slowly, painfully, my dear new friends tried to tell me something. They thought I should get off the train with them – even having no visa. "But I will go to jail without a visa," I said.

"*Besseres*. Warm!"

Yes, at least it would be warm there. No, I mustn't. I have to reach Istanbul to take my boat for Haifa. Already so many days have passed that I shall have almost no time left for Istanbul.

It was late at night when we pulled gently into their deserted station. How sorry I was to see my friends go. Can it be that I had not wanted them to travel in my carriage? They had quite literally saved my life. They had shared their food with me; they had rubbed me to keep my circulation going; they had cheered me. We hugged, exchanged addresses, and cried as if we were a parting family instead of travelers who chanced to meet.

CHAPTER 7

NOW I WAS ALONE. There were no other passengers from the United States on the train. So far, I hadn't even found anybody who could speak English except the conductor, and he was never around. Quite suddenly I felt terribly lonely, lonely and afraid. We had barely covered half the distance from Vienna to Istanbul. Instead of two nights and days on the regular run, it was what? Already three nights — no, this was the fourth! There was no way to know when we would eat again nor how I would keep from freezing.

Surely we are heading south, I thought. Surely it must get warmer. Textbooks tell you that man's greatest drive is to maintain the body temperature, but at that moment I couldn't say which was more important: food or warmth or sleep. I considered the problem for a moment, thinking this was a wonderful opportunity to learn the truth of this concept. But to me they all seemed equally important. What lay ahead I questioned. What else could happen? I shivered with fear and exhaustion. True, I had had that wonderful experience in Vienna and knew that I was not *really* alone. True, I was young and full of confidence and going on my pilgrimage. How could anything bad happen to a pilgrim?

Yet there I was, all by myself, in a politically hostile country, having already been buried by one avalanche, with no heat, and enduring 40°C below zero (according to the thermometer at the station in Sofia), weak from hunger, without lying prone in a bed for what was going on seventy-two hours now, and afraid that any minute the lights might fail completely!

I pulled the seats together, thanking God that I had, at least, bought first-class tickets. The seats made a complete platform which insulated me from the freezing floor. I dug out my spring coat from the suitcase, put it on under my black cape for an extra layer of clothing, and jumped up and down on the red plush platform of the seats to keep from freezing. There was no chubby, warm, and comforting grandmother Stara to rub my arms now; no soft voices murmuring through my drowsiness.

The white basket stood forlornly in the corner. It held only that lonely orange (nobody had wanted to eat it fearing I would need it later) and a few drops of the fiery *arak*. I had closed and locked the door to the compartment and even closed the curtains of the door to protect my meager supplies – now more precious than gold. I was talking out loud to Bahá'u'lláh when suddenly there was a knock at the door.

What should I do? I stopped jumping, my heart pumping with fear. What could I do? Should I answer it? Maybe it was the police! The train made clacking noises. I almost fell as we rounded a bend in the track.

I peeked from a corner of the curtain. In the dim hall there was a young man – slight, dark, with a huge mustache. He wasn't a Bulgar. He had a Middle Eastern look. He also looked impatient as he knocked again. There was nothing else for it but to answer him. "Yes?" I called out.

"You are American?" He was speaking English!

"Yes." What did he want?

"Open the door! I want to speak to you."

"Who are you?"

"A Lebanese student going on holiday from school in England. I want to practice my English."

"It's awfully late. Can't we practice in the morning?"

"It's not yet midnight."

"Are you sure?"

"Open the door. You can't go to sleep in this cold; you'll freeze to death."

That's exactly what I had been afraid of – more afraid of that than of the dark stranger at my door. Maybe the cold would protect me from him. One does foolish things when one is alone: I opened the door.

He stepped back when he saw the platform made

from the seats. "That's a good idea," he admitted. "It gets you off the floor."

He jumped onto my red plush platform. "My name is Karim, and I'm from Beirut." He was dressed in a turtleneck sweater covered by a long overcoat, probably made of camel's hair. He wore some soft leather boots and woolen gloves, but no hat. His eyes were wide and bright with an intelligent expression, open and curious about life. His movements were quick, like a sparrow.

"My name is Jeanne," I told him, "and I'm from Stamford, Connecticut." We sat down cross-legged. "Oh, I wish there were a sleeping car," I sighed.

"There is now. Didn't you feel the jolt? We have joined another section of the Orient Express from Paris."

"Don't tell me that we finally caught the connection that didn't wait for us at Belgrade? I can hardly believe it! They must have been having some problems, too."

"Probably. And then, still another section joined us at the last stop."

"You mean the train is getting longer?"

"Can you believe it?"

"Why don't they inform Paris and Vienna to stop sending the trains through?"

"Well, it is true that many lines are down from the storm, but Sofia doesn't want to inform the 'powers that be,' anyway. They think we'll get through and why should they stop incoming passengers? They need the revenue, I guess."

"That's insane," I whispered.

"That's Bulgaria."

"But if we've caught my train, then maybe I can get into my sleeper? I have my ticket."

"They're all full. They probably sold your compartment when they left Belgrade."

"Oh no! Are you sure? I would buy it back, if necessary. I've just got to get some sleep."

He looked at me intently. "You poor girl. How long has it been since you had a bed?"

"This is the third night. I don't know how much more I can stand."

"Let me see what I can do. I speak German and Turkish. Maybe I can get one for you." Quite forgetting that the *chef de train*, the conductors, and in fact all the personnel of the Orient Express spoke English, I let him go. Hope grew in me as he went off jauntily down the corridor.

We are once more the official Orient Express, I thought, jumping some more to get warm. My legs were tingling, full of needles, so I sat down again to rub them a little.

It was ages before I heard another knock on the door. I must have fallen asleep because I heard the knock insistently but from a long way off. I felt like saying, "Go away, leave me alone," but I didn't. Instead, I moaned.

"Open the door! Open the door!"

"Oh, I'm sorry," I said, struggling up from the

cushions. "I must have dozed off." I opened the door. (Was that door getting heavier?)

"You mustn't go to sleep like that. Wake up! Come with me, I think I've gotten you in."

I was instantly awake. "Wonderful! Shall I take my bags?"

"Yes, bring everything, but hurry. Others are trying to get in." He grabbed my largest suitcase and handed me the smaller one off the rack.

Oddly enough, I was reluctant to leave my compartment. What if we can't get into the sleeping car? I worried to myself. Someone else will have taken my red plush carriage! It was ridiculous, but tears welled up in my eyes. We lurched down the corridor.

"This train is longer than I thought!" I exclaimed after we had passed four cars going forward. Some of them were totally dark – just what I had been worried about. The lights were out.

Finally we came to a locked door. It was completely dark inside. Karim knocked on the door. He knocked again. At last a candle appeared in the window of the door. Somebody behind it was studying us. I heard Karim speak in a strange language – not German, not Bulgarian, not French. My heart was so loud that I could hardly hear them; my arm felt as if it would fall off if I had to carry my things another inch. Even the empty white plastic basket seemed to weigh a ton. My head ached, my feet had no feeling at all. Karim seemed to be arguing with somebody. Oh, what is wrong? I thought.

"Please," I intervened, "please let me buy back my compartment. I haven't much money, but you may have it all."

"It isn't a matter of money, Mademoiselle. There is no room."

My heart sank. Tears again filled my eyes. The light from the candle blinded me. "But I'm so tired. Oh, please find me even an upper berth in a second-class compartment."

Behind the sleeping car attendant, I could hear an authoritative voice call out to him in that strange language. The conductor closed the little window in the locked door.

I looked at Karim. He smiled reassuringly. "Don't worry," he whispered. "You'll get in." I didn't feel all that sure of it myself at the moment. Soon the candlelight appeared in the window again. I could hear a big key scrape in the lock.

"Come in, Mademoiselle. The wife of the Bulgarian ambassador to Turkey will allow you to share her compartment."

"Oh, that's wonderful!" I couldn't help the tears that coursed down my cheeks – tears of relief this time. The attendant took my bags and immediately I felt the 'touch of service' for which the *Compagnie* is so justly famous, even under these incredibly difficult conditions. Still, he wouldn't let Karim in. I turned to wave at him with a wan smile. "Thank you, Karim. Thank you. I'll see you in the morning." He bravely waved from the other side of the door.

"Sleep well, Jeanne Khánum."

I could see dim figures in the candlelight filling the corridor. It was not so cold in here. The heat didn't seem to be working, but for some reason it was warmer. The attendant led me to a dark compartment. The woman in the lower berth was already in bed. There was a steep ladder leading up to the upper berth.

"Just give me a minute, and I'll slip off my boots," I said.

"Pardon, Mademoiselle. There are no sheets on the berth. They must wait until tomorrow. Madame is sleeping," the attendant whispered while he stowed my luggage away. I pulled at the zipper of my boots in the dark.

"That doesn't matter tonight, but if you have a blanket?"

"Right away, Mademoiselle."

The zipper was stiff with the cold. Somehow, standing first on one foot and then the other, I managed to pull my boots off. The attendant handed me a blanket and closed the door as he left.

I felt for the ladder and slowly, painfully, climbed up. My head hit the ceiling, but that didn't matter.

A bed! It was hard and flat. I pulled the blanket up to my chin and was instantly asleep. I didn't awaken again for eleven hours.

CHAPTER
8

WHEN I OPENED MY EYES, the train had stopped again. At first I couldn't remember where I was, but slowly memory came back. The compartment still seemed dark. No, not dark, only dim. The curtains were drawn. I sat up. The woman below was gone. I started down the ladder. It felt sticky. With the curtain open, white light streamed in the window. The rungs of the ladder were stained with a sticky, brown something: I couldn't figure out what. Then I looked at my feet. They were covered with blood.

In confusion, I looked around. There was blood at the foot of the bunk, too. I examined my feet. They were swollen into round balls. When the boots came off, my feet must have broken open – split right open on the bottoms. I knew those boots would never go back on today.

Digging into my large suitcase, I found a blouse and tore it up to wrap around my feet. I thanked mother for my lovely black fur slippers — a present that New Year's.

Hunger drove me to open the door and peer out into the corridor. It was filled with milling passengers. Doors to the different compartments were open and everybody seemed to know everybody else. Maybe, just maybe, I would find something to eat. I ventured into the hall.

"Hello there!" Somebody called to me from the other end of the car. "Come down here, and let us get to know you."

I made my way through the people, limping painfully, but smiling and feeling generally rested and brave once more. Standing in the open door to his compartment was an officer in the uniform of the Turkish army. He was chained with a long, metal cord to some suitcases, so that he couldn't move around very well.

"Good afternoon." He smiled. "I'm Colonel Fathi Mollaglu of Turkish Army Intelligence. Did you sleep well?"

"Oh, yes, thank you. How do you do? I'm Jeanne Bates Frankel."

"Would you like some hot tea?"

"I would *love* some."

Colonel Mollaglu called out in that strange language I had heard the night before, and soon the attendant appeared with a pot of hot steaming tea on a tray.

"I'm afraid there's nothing to eat with it. We've been out of food for more than one day now. But at least it's hot," Fathi told me. The tea was strong and very sweet. It was the most delicious tea I had ever tasted.

I thanked the attendant and asked, "What is your name?"

"Pierre, Mademoiselle. I hope you were comfortable last night."

"Quite, thank you, Pierre. How much do I owe you for my berth?"

"Nothing, Mademoiselle. If you will just give me your ticket, please, which I shall give to the *chef de train* to authorize your stay."

"Of course. Here it is," I said, digging it out of my passport case.

"And you might as well give me your passport now, too. It is hard to say when we shall arrive at the frontier."

"Very well, Pierre . . . and here is five dollars for yourself." He beamed at me.

"I'll put clean sheets on your berth today, now that you're up, Mademoiselle." He went down toward my compartment.

"Well, you certainly made Pierre very happy," the colonel smiled. He was an interesting man, this colonel of the Turkish army. He seemed to be in his forties, of medium build, with gray eyes, and a steady look that said he was accustomed to commanding and getting his orders obeyed. He was apparently well educated and spoke English and French without an accent. He smoked a thin cigarette.

"Why are you attached to these cases?"

"These contain reports gathered from all over Central Europe." His eyes twinkled. "I must get them to Istanbul safely."

"How romantic!" I exclaimed.

Pierre went by on his way to the dining car.

"Pierre, one minute." He stopped.

Oui, Mademoiselle?"

"Where can I find the wife of the Bulgarian ambassador to thank her for letting me into her compartment?"

"It wasn't she," Pierre said. "It was Colonel Mollaglu who ordered me to open the door." He left quietly.

Fathi was smiling at me. I looked at him gratefully. "You can't imagine how much I appreciate this," I told him. I stretched out my feet. Fathi looked at my black slippers stuffed with the white bandages.

"What did you do to your feet?" he asked.

"I guess they were almost frozen," I answered. "They just seemed to break open by themselves."

"How are your fingers?" he asked.

"Swollen and stiff," I answered, "but they are not bleeding."

"You're lucky at that. There are others on this train who are in a more pitiable condition."

I felt suddenly chastened. "Oh, that's terrible! We

must do something for them. Are there any doctors on board?"

"Not as far as we can tell. Of course, it has been rather difficult for me to move around." He smiled apologetically.

"Don't worry," I replied. "I'll go and find out. But what will I do about the language? You and Karim seem to be the only people on board who speak English, besides the staff of the train."

"Well, your Karim speaks Turkish and Arabic as well as English and German. I heard him last night speaking everything trying to get Pierre to open the door. That is, he spoke everything but French, and I'll just bet he speaks that, too," Fathi laughed. "Karim really pleaded your case at that door." He sobered a little. "You will need somebody to speak Bulgarian and Rumanian as well as . . . let me see, probably Hungarian."

"Goodness! Do you think we can find all that?"

"Of course." He rang for the attendant.

"*Oui, Monsieur?*" Pierre asked when he arrived on the run.

"Who is in this car that speaks Rumanian, and perhaps Hungarian?" Fathi asked.

"Well, Monsieur, there is the ambassador from Rumania to Turkey in the compartment next to yours."

"You mean the man who keeps sticking his nose out and then ducking back into his room?"

"*Oui, Monsieur.*" (Fathi grinned at me.) "And then

there is a Hungarian dancer in the next first-class coach," Pierre concluded.

"Well, we can't put the Bulgarian ambassador together with the Rumanian ambassador. They don't speak to each other. But perhaps the wife of the Bulgarian ambassador will be more diplomatic."

"This looks like quite a gathering," I said.

I found Karim two cars to the rear, huddled into a corner. He looked cold and so tired. I shook him by the shoulder. "Wake up!" I said. "We have work to do." I explained the plan. He sleepily agreed to be my main translator.

"What can you do for them, Jeanne?"

"I don't know. But I'm an old 'jungle nurse,' although it's been years since I practiced. Still something is better than nothing. Let's go."

We worked our way back to the sleeping car. The attendant let us both in, and we met the other members of our 'medical caravan' at Fathi's compartment. The Lady Ambassador from Bulgaria, Aida Rostova, spoke limited French. She must have been between fifty and sixty years old. She was short and chubby and wore her hair pulled back into a knot. I thanked her for receiving me into her compartment, which she acknowledged with quiet reserve. She smiled shyly at me.

There was a girl of dark, brooding beauty standing by Fathi. He introduced her as Gabriella Duli, a dancer from Hungary. Her long, thick, black hair hung in heavy waves around her face. Her eyes were almost as black as her hair, with thick lashes heavily made up. Her teeth were white and bright when she smiled. Her skin had a yellowish tinge. She wore high boots of some shiny material and a rather short skirt. Over this she wore a bulky jacket of long-haired, light-colored fur, marked with irregular spots. Her engagement to dance at a club in Budapest had been cancelled because of the storms, and she was *en route* to Istanbul – and due to open there tomorrow. She would be very late.

Next to them stood Ambassador Bretean, from Rumania. He was slight of build with dark, curly hair and a somewhat withdrawn manner. He was definitely not a gregarious personality. But he spoke German and French and would prove to be a big help with all the Jewish refugees on the train who were bound for Israel and who spoke Rumanian.

There was one more person standing in the crowded entrance to Fathi's compartment: the *chef de train*, André Morand, very definitely French. He was older than the others and wore gold-rimmed glasses which he tended to look over, rather than through. He had a thin, sharp face and a calm and quiet manner with an air of one accustomed to being obeyed. He had been with the *Compagnie* for many years and ran his train with quiet authority. Nonetheless, he was very polite and courteous.

Fathi explained the need for translators and it worked out very well. Ambassador Bretean and

Gabriella would translate their languages into German, and then Karim would take over and translate from German into English. Madame Rostova would translate directly into French, which I should be able to handle by myself. Karim, again, would handle all the Middle Eastern tongues. It sounded confusing, but we were pleased to have covered all the bases so easily. "Maybe we'll find a doctor?" I said hopefully, in English and French, which Karim repeated in German. We were off!

Meanwhile, Fathi and the *chef de train* were consulting on the conditions in the train. I overheard Monsieur Morand saying, ". . . many mountains between here and the coast. It is hard to say what we shall encounter . . ."

The medical caravan started at the very beginning of the train and worked its way back to the last car. The conditions were even more appalling than I had imagined — especially in the common cars added from the different countries *en route*. There were second-class, and even third-class coaches, some with only wooden benches, and in those cars the suffering was the worst. There was shock, particularly among the older passengers. Most of the children seemed to be running a fever. Several were actually retching from hunger. And who knew what we were yet to face? There were virtually no sanitary facilities, for the pipes had all frozen and the toilets were a disaster.

Admittedly there was now a dining car, but the kitchen had no food. Still, we could gather clean snow and make hot water and tea. There was still some sugar left.

Gabriella was particularly good with the children, and each member of the medical team was affected by the pitiful situation of our fellow passengers. Finally, we went back to our own sleeping car and sat down with Fathi to make plans.

He looked grim. "The train is in worse condition than I thought," he said. "The weather, too, is worsening in front of us, and the daily arrival of more cars makes the situation very serious indeed. The *chef de train* says we have almost four hundred passengers on board now. Did you find a doctor?"

"No. Isn't that surprising? No medical people at all. What first aid supplies do we have?"

Just then the train lurched slowly forward. Fathi rang the bell and sent Pierre off to find the *chef de train*, Monsieur Morand. When he arrived, we asked him to gather all the medical supplies he could from the train itself, and to ask the conductors to go among the passengers requesting that they surrender all medicines, spirits, perfumes, and colognes for the common good. Monsieur Morand gave us one of the first-class, non-sleeping cars, which we began to wipe down with as much alcohol as we could spare. Never will I forget the Lady Ambassador, Madame Rostova, with a sheet tied around her, bent over making up beds and scrubbing window ledges.

When everything was gathered, the supplies were pitiful indeed. We had aspirin, about 2,000 tablets, for fever. We had a few bottles of vitamin C – not very high milligrams, but something. We had several assorted antibiotics – about fifty capsules of 250 milligrams each. Then we had a shelf of liquors, mostly *arak* and *slivovitz*, for sterilizing. Finally, we had seven lemons and my single orange from the white basket. There was nothing for serious illness, but it would have to do. I thought the worst thing we would have to treat would be the effects of hunger, particularly in the aged and the children. I was wrong.

We settled the most serious 'cases' into our hospital car. I suspected that many of the ladies had not surrendered their colognes, nor their patent medicines, but there was no way to force them. Maybe if the need arose, they would volunteer them. Pierre brought tea to all the patients and the medical caravan, so I left Karim in charge and went back to the sleeping car to have tea with Fathi. My feet were throbbing, and they had begun to bleed again. The train stopped again with a jolt.

It was growing dark and the wind picked up once more, fulfilling the prophecy about the worsening weather. But I felt better knowing that we had done what we could.

"Jeanne, while you're here," he said, "let me chain you to these papers while I go, ah, down the hall for a moment." Fathi took a small key from his pocket and unlocked his handcuff.

"Chain *me* to them?" I smiled. "But you barely know me. Maybe I'm a spy or something."

"Not you. Besides you're American. We're on the same side." I smiled to myself. Here I was, chained to the secret papers of the Turkish army, sipping hot tea, on the Orient Express to Istanbul. What would happen next?

Just then I had my answer. There was a terrible crash. Hot tea spilled over my hand, burning it. Fathi came running back, excited. "Are you all right?" he asked.

"Yes." I said. "What was that?"

"I'm not sure. It feels like we hit something." He grabbed a conductor who was hurrying through.

"Come, please, there's been an accident," said the conductor, looking at me.

"Right away," I agreed. Fathi unlocked the handcuff around my wrist. "But what has happened? The train stopped about a half hour ago. How could we have hit anything?"

"The engine was trying to break free from a small snowdrift, Mademoiselle," the conductor (not Pierre) said, leading me through the crowd. "A man has been injured."

I thought that the engine must have hit the man, but no. When we arrived, one car from our hospital car, there he sat, on the floor of the corridor. His head was covered with blood. An icy blast from the window above him showed the cracked glass and the break his head had made in it.

Quickly, I examined him. He had split his head open as easily as my feet had opened. "This will have to be sewn up," I murmured. "Find Karim," I said to the conductor.

With help from some of the passengers, I got the man to his feet and into our hospital car. He seemed dazed and confused. Karim soon arrived, and I explained what had to be done. We had no surgical thread, of course, but we had to do something before the pain really set in. Karim spoke to him in German. He seemed to understand, because he didn't make a move when I poured *arak* into the wound to clean any fragments of glass out of it. Karim had opened some of the antibiotic capsules, and we poured the powder directly into the wound. One of the ladies, I think it was Gabriella, provided a sewing needle and thread — white, fortunately. The conductor held a flashlight because by now there was virtual darkness.

I soaked the needle in *arak*, burned it, and then quite simply stitched the flesh together. Meanwhile, Karim tore a sheet into bandages. We made a pressure pad and wrapped up the man's head. We gave him two of our precious antibiotic capsules to swallow and told his wife (in German) to give him one every four hours. I dug deep into my case and came up with a small bottle of Demerol painkillers, given to me by some doctor for something or other — I could no longer remember. We gave the man one and left him to his wife.

It was quite late when we finished. Back in my own compartment, I fell into a deep sleep. (Was I dreaming or was there the sound of guitar music in the background?)

Sometime later, still night, I awakened to the sound of the turning wheels. We were moving once more. It was difficult to keep track of when the train stopped and started again. We still couldn't move with any speed, but we were moving. At times it seemed we would never reach our destination. Where were we now? I didn't know. It was too dark to read, so I crept quietly down the ladder and slipped out of the compartment and down the hall. The door to Fathi's compartment was shut, so I went on by it and through to the dining car. Four Austrian businessmen were playing cards in a cloud of cigar smoke. The dining car attendant was missing, so I looked for him.

In the kitchen area, between high stacks of shelves, were a couple of hammocks. In one of them was the missing attendant, and in the other was a giant of a man with a black beard. I guessed that he was our *chef de cuisine*, practically out of work for lack of anything to cook. I left quietly. They, too, deserved to rest.

Back in the restaurant car, at a table for two in one corner, sat Gabriella. An ashtray was overflowing in front of her, and she was strumming a guitar. The haunting music was a fitting accompaniment to the howling wind and mournful night. She didn't look up.

There was no conversation for me here. What a strange little world we were.

I wound my way back through the sleeper to the other end of the car. Pierre was dozing at his little table by the door. He didn't awaken as I passed. I unlocked the door and went into the ordinary coaches. Everything was quiet in our hospital car. Karim was asleep on one of the platforms we had made for the children. At least these few passengers had blankets. I looked fondly at him. He had his arm around a little boy. The child looked peaceful in his sleep, the pinched look of hunger erased by rest.

Satisfied that everything was quiet, even better than could be expected under the circumstances, I returned to my own compartment. The thing that kept me in wonder was the marvelous way everybody was working together. People from different countries, ideologies, religions, and with every possible barrier standing between them – even language – in the face of common need had overcome these differences to work for the good of all. It was an inspiring thought. There was very little pettiness and no greed. But why do people have to reach the brink of death to exhibit these qualities? How can people be encouraged to keep their unity and their cooperation under normal conditions? I sighed. But, that's why Bahá'u'lláh came, I suppose. *"O my God! O my God! Unite the hearts of Thy servants, and reveal to them Thy great purpose..."* The prayer lulled me back to sleep.

CHAPTER

9

EARLY THE NEXT MORNING we crossed into Greece. The storm had let up and spirits were high. Greece was a free country. We had passed through the intangible, but very real, iron curtain. All through the cars there was a feeling of release. Smiles came more easily and even hunger was forgotten as the passengers strained to look out the windows onto this ancient land where democracy was born.

The medical caravan tended the forty or so patients in the hospital car. I changed the bandages of the Rumanian man with the head wound. Marvel of marvels, there was no infection. "Thank God, he's robust and strong," I told Karim. Later making our rounds of the rest of the cars, we were surprised to find seven people with symptoms suspiciously like appendicitis. "Well, that's all we would need," I grumbled to Karim as we finished examining the seventh patient doubled up with pain. "Why the sudden flare-up?"

"God only knows, Jeanne."

"Well, it's beyond *my* medical knowledge. Maybe it's just the extreme hardships they are enduring on this journey." We moved them all into the hospital car, which was now crowded with nearly fifty patients. We made more platforms from the seats so that we could squeeze more people into each compartment and remade the platforms with the now dubiously clean sheets. It seemed better not to look at them too closely.

Pierre and two other conductors brought trays of hot tea (which looked weaker by the day) and one old lady got the orange. We were afraid we would lose her if we tried to save it any longer. She had no teeth, but her smile was brave.

Very soon we crossed into Turkey, but the train didn't stop. We passed a little wayside station in front of some shabby shacks. I went down to give Fathi a break from his chain and asked, "Why didn't we stop at the border?"

"You'll see, Jeannie, pretty soon we shall be back in Greece."

He made off for the W.C. and I couldn't help wondering what he had done before I arrived on the scene. We hardly knew each other well enough to mention it, but I couldn't resist. "Fathi," I asked, when he returned refreshed and neat in his uniform, which never seemed to need pressing. "Tell me, how . . . no, who wore the handcuff before Pierre let me into this car?"

Fathi's eyes twinkled. "Well, now, I shouldn't say. But haven't you noticed that Monsieur Morand, the *chef de train*, has been particularly nice to you?"

Monsieur Morand was so dignified. The thought of him chained to those papers brought peals of laughter from us both. We couldn't stop. I guess it was just pent-up emotion coming out.

Almost before we knew it we were back in Greece. This was the first time this had ever happened to me – to cross into the country of destination and out of it again, never once stopping. But this time we had a two-hour stopover at the little Greek border station.

I couldn't refuse a chance to get off the train to visit with the border guards. What a difference between Greece and Bulgaria! These guards were so casual and relaxed. Their guardhouse was a shack really, but there was a warm round-bellied stove. Very sweet black coffee sat bubbling on the top. Two guards were sitting, their feet on the edge of the stove, smoking something really foul smelling. They kindly offered me a tiny cup of the coffee. It gave me the hiccups. They laughed uproariously. One of the guards, looking fierce with his black hair and huge mustache, but smiling at me, handed me a tiny piece of hard candy made with honey. It was so good that it brought tears to my eyes. Why couldn't the train be stuck here for a while? I thought. But no, there went the whistle. I realized that it had blown very seldom on this trip. Back to the filthy, freezing, dark, and dingy train. How could I still love to travel by train? I must be nuts.

The final border crossing came at a town in Turkey called Edirne. I was sitting with Fathi when the border guards came through. They saluted him smartly, and carelessly took my passport, opening it quickly. Not looking at what he was doing, one of the guards brought out a large stamp and, before I could stop him – bang! Down came the inked stamp, right on top of my precious visa to the Cocos-Keeling islands. This was an almost impossible-to-obtain visa, and, more importantly, one of the goals of the Ten-Year World Crusade, which mother and I had opened to the Faith.

"Oh, no! This is too much," I wailed, as tears of frustration and distress welled up in my eyes. The guards were apologetic, but it was done. They left with a shrug. I openly wept. Wept from tiredness and hunger. Wept for my treasured visa. Wept from the impossibilities of this terrible journey. Fathi tried to comfort me, but he didn't understand. How could he? Nobody could understand. "A pilgrimage shouldn't be like this!" I blurted out. Later I was to remember that moment with shame.

Edirne was a big port city and, although we couldn't see much of it, we stopped there long enough to drop off the extra engines we had gathered along the way from the new trains coming through daily. It seemed to me that we needed these engines to break through the small snowdrifts on the tracks. But maybe now the worst was over. So far, every time I had a thought like that, I had been wrong.

Still, the officials at the train station in Edirne gave us hope. They called ahead to a small town on the route, told them of our plight, and the townspeople agreed to have bread and soup ready for us when the train arrived. I couldn't understand why they didn't just feed us there at Edirne. That was one mystery that was never to be solved.

The news of food cheered the whole train immensely. Even the patients picked up at the thought. Secretly, Fathi and I weren't too enthusiastic. How could they feed so many? we pondered.

About two hours after the border crossing, the train slowed to a crawl. I heard shouting and looked out the window. Four sets of rails showed through the snow outside the window. People were lining the track with huge, round loaves of bread in their outstretched hands. The women were dressed in long skirts, shirtlike blouses, and shawls, with their heads covered in scarves. The men looked more like ruffians than rescuers, with unshaved faces and homespun clothes. Some wore what looked like sheepskins made into vests, over which were belts of leather stuffed with bullets for the long rifles they carried. A cheer went up!

Windows came down all along the train, and wretched hands reached out to grab the bread. The town was called Alpulu, and the people waiting for us were smiling, laughing, happy to be of help.

The mayor or elder of the village was waiting to receive us when the train came to a stop. It was a typical Balkan wayside station, not raised, but level with the ground, so that there was a deep step down from the train. A few chickens pecked around the long, flat-roofed building behind the tracks.

The *chef de train* opened the door of our carriage first so that we could arrange to feed the sick and injured before the other descending passengers could block the entrances. I went into the large central room of the station and immediately made for the Ladies' Room. This certainly disproved the theory that the first of man's needs is food. Finally I had solved the dilemma. It wasn't food or body temperature, it was the need for a clean toilet.

What I found left me helpless with laughter. It was clean, it had a nice door that I could close, but there wasn't any kind of toilet. There was only a hole in the floor, nicely tiled, with convenient little places for one's feet. I had grown up with this kind of thing in the Far East, and so finding one of these 'Asian toilets' in this rest stop in Turkey made me realize, as nothing else could, that we were finally in the Orient. What struck me so funny was: with all these clothes on, how could one use it? Slacks, slippers, coats, cape: how would one get them off and out of the way? The impossibility of the situation struck me so funny that I rushed out of the toilet and back to the train, doubled over with laughter.

Pierre looked at me with puzzlement. I couldn't speak. I pushed my way past the crowds in the corridor and into our smelly, waterless W.C. It was not clean, but it was furnished with a beautiful, ordinary seat!

My laughter controlled, and necessities attended to, I returned to the station to receive a frown from our host, the mayor. I smiled my apology, and we began a serving line into the hospital car for those too weak to move.

The soup was delicious, rich, and nourishing. It even had pieces of meat – lamb – really chunks, and it was thick with some kind of white bean. There were delicate spices, and the best thing of all was that it was hot. It was the first hot food most of us had eaten for six days. I give it full credit for saving many lives.

All of us had forgotten how swollen our fingers had become, and when the bread cooled, the crust became very hard. Wonderful and tasty but difficult to break. Our fingers broke open first with the effort to tear the bread apart. And our gums bled, but there wasn't a single person there who worried about that! Never have I tasted bread that good, before or since.

Car by car, the passengers went into the building and quietly stood in line for two or three bowls of soup. We had to limit them to that, for they had been fasting so long that any more food would have only increased the illnesses. They ate their soup with bread soaking in it and quietly returned to the train. Gabriella played her guitar for us, adding much to the festivity of the banquet. There was a feeling of normality in the air. People laughed and sang. The children played and smiled. Eyes danced, hope soared. Even the Bulgarian ambassador, Monsieur Rostov, was smiling and, for once, didn't bully his wife. Surely the worst is over, I thought. There I went again, thinking that. Again I was wrong.

CHAPTER
10

THE TRAIN PULLED OUT of Alpulu as the sun set behind the mountains. A rosy glow covered the white countryside. We all felt warm and sleepy. The train moved faster and faster across the relatively flat land, and then more slowly and with greater effort when it started up the mountains again. The engine whistled, a new kind of whistle, the brave, strong blast of a Greek engine driver. Up and around we went. Then the locomotive labored, with the rasping breath of a dying dragon. Each long, heavy breath seemed to be the last it would draw, but then came another.

Suddenly, with a horrible grating noise that awakened everyone, the train came to a stop – this time a stop with a sharp, hard jolt.

I sat up and hit my head on the ceiling of my compartment. Oh, not again! I thought. Down the ladder, out into the hall, when a knock came at the door to the sleeping car. It was Karim. This time the door was opened immediately, for he had become well known in this car.

"Another avalanche," he said. "Or maybe it's a huge snowdrift. Anyway, we've hit it. It's too dark to see how bad the damage is."

We gathered our medical team together. The train struggled to free itself, while we went through the cars to see if any of the passengers had been hurt. Remarkably few, we learned with surprise. There were some bumped heads: we gave them aspirin. There had been a couple of falls: again, we gave them aspirin. There was a lot of fear: and we also gave them aspirin. Then the lights went out completely.

What little power we had was gone. The engine died. Terror gripped our hearts as a terrible silence filled the train. This had never happened before throughout the whole trip. At least we had always had the comforting sound of the panting locomotive – our black dragon. Now it had been slain!

The *chef de train*, taking a couple of the conductors, opened a door to go forward to see about the engine. Karim and I peered out into the darkness. Strangely enough there was a moon, streaked by dark clouds to be sure, but a moon. The wind whistled and beat us with icy cold.

We jumped out onto the snow and sank into it almost up to our waists. All along the train, doors were opening and people were looking for clean spots to substitute for those infamous toilets. Suddenly, we heard clearly from a distance the high, thin howling of wolves. I shivered and turned to Karim. "Let's go back. It's positively eerie out here." He agreed and helped me back onto the train.

Just then a conductor came up. "Follow me, mademoiselle. There is a problem in the prison car."

"The prison car?" I asked him.

"Yes, the one nearest the engine."

"But we haven't even been in there yet. I thought that car was used for luggage."

That's true, we do put luggage into it. But this trip we had a load of prisoners, and we had to put them somewhere."

"They must be frozen. Did they have any food at Alpulu?" I asked.

"I don't know. There is another conductor there and, of course, the guards who are in charge of them," he replied. "Come quickly, please. It is better if we go forward from the outside: it is faster."

I doubted that, remembering how we had just jumped into snow almost up to our waists. But the conductor took us out on the other side, in the lee of the storm, where a narrow strip of cleared land left a path to follow. We could see the wall of snow blocking the way of the train, and I began to doubt that we would ever leave this spot. Karim and I exchanged glances.

The prison car almost defied description. The walls were slatted, and here and there air came through them.

The floor was bare wood. Naturally, there was absolutely no heat. Even the guards looked almost dead, their faces drawn and gray. But the prisoners – the prisoners were filthy and chained to the wall. Many of them were unable even to sit down. The odor, in spite of the cold, was appalling.

We were met by another conductor. Our breath fell heavily in frosty crystals as we spoke.

"Have these men eaten?" I asked indignantly.

"They have had bread and one bowl of soup each," he replied defensively. "That is when I discovered the problem."

"What is it?" I said, thinking that everything here was a problem, and one which we weren't going to solve with aspirin.

The conductor held a flashlight toward one of the prisoners who was standing with his head against the wall. "Look at this man's hand, mademoiselle."

At first I thought that it was just because the man was so dirty and the light was so bad that the hand looked so dark. I gagged when I went nearer to him. His eyes were not hostile – they didn't have enough life in them to be hostile, but the smell . . .

"What's the matter with it?" I asked. The conductor pointed to the hand that was chained to the wall. There was a thick red welt around the wrist where the metal handcuff held him. Then I looked more closely. The hand was black! Was it frozen? I thought in horror. It was puffy and swollen and had a strange texture. I had never seen a frozen hand before. My stomach turned over. There was a putrid odor coming from it, and streaks of red went up the wrist to the arm. I recoiled in disgust. Karim caught me as I literally backed into him. "That hand has got to come off," I told Karim in a low voice. "I must see it in better light." I turned to the conductor. "You must remove their handcuffs."

"That is impossible, Mademoiselle."

"We'll see about that!" I felt defiant. Fathi would help them. "In the meantime, you must bring this man into the hospital car."

"He will escape, Mademoiselle. There is no way to keep him in there."

"He won't escape," I assured him. "He's much too ill to escape. Furthermore, if you don't do something to help the rest of these wretched men, they'll all be dead before we reach Istanbul." Karim made sure that the conductor heard that in Turkish as well as English, and there was a stir among the prisoners. I turned to leave. I couldn't get away from that horror chamber fast enough.

Back in the hospital car, I asked Karim to get the prisoner some very hot, sweet tea. The least I could do for him was to get his blood sugar up and warm him as much as possible. Pierre helped me make up a bed and found some blankets to cover him. One of the guards had won the toss and had come with him. I told him to stay out of the way and left to return to my own car.

There were no lights whatsoever throughout the whole train. I had to feel my way along the corridors until finally the candlelight still flickering in the window of my sleeper appeared. I looked at that tiny beacon. It was pitifully small, almost burned out. I knocked at Fathi's door.

"Come in. I'm not asleep," he called out to me. He must have known from my steps in the corridor who it was.

"Oh, Fathi, what in heaven are we going to do?" Quickly I told him what I had found.

"I'll think of something to do about the other prisoners, but that hand sounds like it's got to be amputated," he said grimly.

"Oh, but Fathi, I can't do it! I've never done anything like that before. He'll die! I'm just not qualified enough. Oh, why wasn't there a doctor at Alpulu?"

"In Turkey many smaller towns are served by visiting physicians. There just aren't enough people in one small village to support a trained man."

"Oh, I know that. I didn't mean to criticize that. But I can't do it. I just can't!"

"Jeanne, now calm down. There isn't anybody else. No one else here has any medical training at all. I'll try to do everything I can to help you. Now think clearly." He rang the bell. "Pierre, it's time to bring out that bottle of cognac you've been hiding."

"*Oui, Monsieur.*" He ducked out and was back in a

minute with a bottle of old French cognac and two glasses.

Fathi thanked him, pulled the cork, and filled one of the little bulbous glasses to the rim. "Here, drink this," he ordered me. "We've been saving this for a really big problem."

"Oh, Fathi, I shouldn't, and you shouldn't have." I shivered with nerves.

"Yes, you will. Now drink it!" He pushed the glass into my hand. I took it. The cognac was warming and soothing.

"I'm sorry, Bahá'u'lláh. Don't be cross with me. It's really medicine," I prayed. Of course Bahá'u'lláh wouldn't be 'cross,' what a foolish thing to pray. I was cross with myself for being so weak and silly.

Fathi started in again: "Now, have you thought about what you are going to need?"

"Well, light is the main thing. I can't see well enough to do anything like that in the hospital car. It's too dark."

"Can we wait until morning?"

"I don't know. I don't think so," I said. "It's already gangrenous. I don't even know if I can save his life." I shook my head with uncertainty.

"Now don't think like that," he tried to reassure me. "What else do you need?"

"Some place where I can do it. The hospital car just won't work from many points of view. We need a table: some place where I can at least stand up straight and not have to bend over him."

"The dining room then."

"And I'll need a knife." I shuddered. "A sharp 1 knife."

Then I had a terrible thought. "Oh dear God! Fathi, it won't work. I have nothing to cut through the bone. And what's more, I don't have the strength to do it."

"You'll do it," he said firmly. "We'll ask the *chef de cuisine* to help you. He's a husky fellow; together you'll do it."

"What about an anesthetic?"

"We don't have any. We'll have to use whiskey."

"You mean *arak*. But that could be dangerous," I protested.

"Well then?"

"I don't know." Just then Karim came in.

"Your patient is feverish, I think, Jeanne. But he's more comfortable, at least." Fathi handed him a glass of the cognac.

"Karim," I said, "make the rounds again. Ask all the passengers if there is anything at all that they have that we might use as an anesthetic — anything. And please find Monsieur Morand and send him to us."

"OK, but what are you going to do?"

"We're going to amputate," Fathi said.

"Whew!" Karim whistled. He tossed off his drink and went off shaking his head.

When Monsieur Morand arrived, we told him our plans. He nodded, looked at us over his glasses, said nothing, and left to arrange the dining car. That means that the Austrians will have to stop playing cards, I thought. I sighed. "Fathi, I wish you could be there with us?"

"You know that's impossible, Jeanne Khánum. You'll do just fine." I followed Monsieur Morand out of the car.

It was getting very late, or maybe it was really very early in the morning, by the time everything was as ready as we could make it.

All the flashlights we could muster were ready to be trained on the table the attendants had prepared in the dining car. They had placed two dining tables together to make one long operating table big enough for the tall man who would soon trust his life to us on it. They had covered this first with a blanket and then with clean tablecloths. It looked quite suitable. A potbellied stove was burning brightly for warmth and also to sterilize the knives. Where had that stove been hiding?

I had shed my black cape, and the chef loaned me a big apron which wrapped around me and a large white towel to tie around my hair. The chef also had water boiling and was brewing up a preparation of herbs. Karim had gathered them from a Rumanian traveler who swore that the tea made from these leaves would put the patient to sleep. I strongly doubted that, but if it didn't work, I was going to give him Demerol. I couldn't trust the *arak* treatment.' Besides, I was sure that everybody was giving him swigs of the yellow firewater whenever my back was turned. He already had a glassy look in his eyes, and nothing was budging that fever. He was burning up!

Gabriella had opened about ten of the antibiotic capsules and made a small pile of the powder to pour onto the wound after we finished. We kept that in a sterilized little cup by the table.

We put the knives into the fire and when they brought the patient to the table, he climbed onto it by himself. Karim gave him the strong herbal mixture and spoke softly to him in what I supposed was Turkish. His eyes took on a look of pure terror when he looked at the knives heating in the stove.

We shaved his arm and washed it – no, scrubbed it, in *arak*, then hot water and a small sliver of soap, and rinsed it again in *arak*. We cut his fingernails and did whatever we could to remove the worst of the corruption from the surface. By this time, I was astonished to see his eyes close. He fell into a deep sleep. Beads of perspiration covered his face. The herbal tea must have worked. Nobody believed that it would work through the pain of the operation, but at least he was asleep for now.

Finally, I ordered the flashlights turned on. The sturdiest men the chef could find stood outside the circle of light and held those flashlights very steady. They were strong-nerved men from the mountains. Their faces were lined with suffering and hardship. The wind howled outside as a new storm built out of the night. We could still hear the wolves calling in the hills – and somehow they seemed nearer. There was no way to postpone the thing any longer.

The chef handed me a long kitchen knife which was to be our scalpel. I made an incision across the wrist. A thin line of blood showed on the skin; the patient didn't move. Could it be that there was a natural anesthetic at work here? I wondered. The knife cut deeper. Karim wiped the blood away. Our sponges were primitive in the extreme. I tried to be as careful as possible. The best thing was to cut straight and get the hand at the wrist, hoping we could prevent the infection from spreading up the arm. There were no clamps.

Almost immediately, I felt the resistance of bone. I looked at the chef. "I am here, Mademoiselle."

"Check my angle. Do you think I've hit the joint?" I asked anxiously.

"It looks good to me, Mademoiselle. It is rather like cutting up a leg of meat for the soup." His words were muffled because I had forced him to cover that black beard with a towel.

"That's a terrible thing to say! I hope not." I shuddered involuntarily. "Help me. We've got to get through this cartilage and bone."

"Allow me." He took the knife out of my hand and, with a grunt, pushed down hard. The hand rolled off the table! Blood spurted everywhere.

"Good! Now quick, give me the other knife!" I cried.

They brought the second knife out of the fire – red hot!

"Give it to me," I almost screamed.

I held the flat edge of the knife to the bloody stub of a wrist. There was a searing noise as the blood bubbled on the red-hot steel. With a scream, the patient woke up!

"Hold him now!" I yelled, continuing to sear the wound. I was perspiring and sweat poured into my eyes. My thoughts were praying to God for help. The patient was screaming, his eyes bulging out of his head. I took the knife away. A seared stub was left. We poured the antibiotic powder over the stump. The patient passed out. We made a thick pad and bandaged the arm.

Six men carried him back to the hospital car. They were to stand guard with him all the rest of the night. I gave them Demerol for him to take when he awakened. I was sure he was going to die. Oh, God, I thought, he's in your hands now!

When I left him in the hospital car, I started to tremble violently. I could hardly walk back to my own car. What a sight I must have been when I reached Fathi's compartment. He handed me the cognac. "Take a big swallow," he ordered. I took one and fainted.

CHAPTER
11

THE NEXT MORNING, I awakened in my own compartment. But Madame Rostova was in the upper berth and I was in the lower one. I felt amazingly well after the ordeal of the night before. My dreams had seemed to be one long repeated prayer, a hangover from the constant praying of the day before – the very best kind of hangover in the world.

How had I reached my compartment? I couldn't remember. I sat up and felt gingerly for my feet. The swelling seemed better. I peeked out from behind the curtain. The sun was shining. There was nothing in sight: no houses, no roads or telephone lines, no animals, not even a bird. Just miles and miles of empty countryside. I could see the train stretching out from behind and to the front, and I wondered if more cars had joined us during the night. Somehow, I didn't think so. There was no new locomotive behind us. That was a good sign. There were men working around the engine. Some of them held shovels, and all of them were moving around. At least something was happening.

Hurriedly, I smoothed my badly wrinkled clothes, brushed through my hair, and used some lipstick on my sore, cracked lips. I was a mess. How long has it been since I've had a bath? I thought. Thank heavens for deodorants and baby powder!

I was hungry again. Maybe I could still find some tea. With the sun out, everything seemed more optimistic. The door to Fathi's compartment was open: he looked weary and badly in need of a shave.

"Good morning, Fathi. Did you sleep?"

"More to the point, did you sleep?" he asked.

"I can't remember a thing after you gave me the cognac."

"You were really out," Fathi laughed. "We carried you back to your compartment, but we couldn't manage the ladder. So our Lady Ambassador had to climb up." We giggled, thinking of her heavy weight mounting that ladder.

"I'm starving, Fathi. Do you think there might still be some of that wonderful bread from Alpulu left?"

"We'll find out. But first, let me go down the hall." He exchanged the handcuff and staggered rather than walked to the W.C. at the end of the hall. His eyes, which usually looked so alive and penetrating, somehow seemed very tired and dull. The lack of food is getting to him, I thought. This is more difficult for him than for the rest of us, having to stay constantly with these papers. At least we are able to move around, but Fathi can only go to the end of his chain. Why, he's as much a prisoner as those miserable men in the baggage car! I rang for the attendant. I wondered what they did to solve the problem of where to put those men.

Just then Pierre answered the bell. *"Bonjour, Mademoiselle."*

"Pierre, would you please bring two pots of tea, and perhaps a bit of bread?"

"Immédiatement, Mademoiselle." He seemed bright this morning. Could it be that he really still had some of the bread? I wondered.

Fathi came back looking somewhat refreshed — at least he had shaved. Although almost all of the men in our little stranded world were growing beards for warmth and comfort, Fathi wasn't. It was a mystery to me how he managed to shave.

"My, that was quick! I've ordered tea, and even bread. Pierre didn't say no." Fathi changed the handcuff once more, and I suddenly felt very sorry for him. "Do you have a large family, Fathi?" I asked, somehow feeling a bit shy.

"I certainly do." He smiled proudly and pulled out a wallet stuffed with photos of five beautiful children, all with those great big eyes. "The eldest is ten and the youngest is only three." A really gorgeous woman sat in the middle of them.

"Is this your wife?"

"Shookoh, she's Iranian."

I sighed. It was a small world. "Oh, Fathi, do you think we will ever reach Istanbul alive?"

"Certainly we will."

"But it seems nobody cares what happens to us. I mean, at Edirne for example, if they knew what the road ahead of us was like, why did they permit us to continue?"

"You have to remember, Jeanne, that the lines of communication are somewhat chancy during the winter. Probably, when we were there everything was all right up to Istanbul. Storms can build very quickly in these hills." Just then, Pierre arrived with a tray and, sure enough, there was a plate of hot bread. Behind him came Monsieur Morand.

"Join us, Monsieur *chef de train*," Fathi said. Now, on Turkish territory, Fathi was the ranking passenger. Monsieur Morand took off his hat and sat down. "Another cup for Monsieur, Pierre."

"*Oui, mon colonel.*" Pierre hurried off.

"Well, what is the situation, Monsieur?"

"Well, *mon colonel*, zer ees some progress. We have established work crews, using some of zee prisoners to augment my staff. Zey are taking turns at using zee shovels to try to free zee engine." He spoke English in deference to me, I was sure. "But it ees slow work," he continued, his strong accent turning his words into a lilting song. "We have to change zee teams of workers every twenty minutes or zey will get zee frostbite on zee hands and noses."

"Is it true, Monsieur Morand," I interjected, "that no new cars have joined the train since we left Alpulu?"

"*Oui, Mademoiselle.* Zat ees true."

"Well, that's a relief," I said. "At the very least, it shows that in Paris and Vienna the *Compagnie* knows there is trouble here."

"*Mais oui! C'est vrai, Mademoiselle.* And een Istanbul, too. You can be very sure zey are taking zee steps for our rescue. Help is most assuredly on zee way at zeess very moment."

"What else is being done, Monsieur Morand?" asked Fathi.

"It ees why I came to consult wees you, *mon colonel.*"

"Well, we certainly have to establish other work crews as well. You have done the right thing to begin work on the most important problem, that is, freeing the engine. But it could take days, and we must consider the need for food and . . ."

"And sanitary facilities," I interrupted. "Those toilets could cause very serious health complications." I was thinking of typhoid, but not wanting to say it.

"Zat ees true, Mademoiselle. Of course, zer would be even more of a problem if zee weazer were warmer. But still, we must do somezing."

"I suggest, Monsieur Morand," Fathi said, "that you appoint work crews to take some shovels and bury the mess in the snow. The men can take turns. It should be done twice a day, weather permitting." I shuddered thinking about them. "Then, too," Fathi continued. "we shall need teams of men to gather snow to melt for cleaning and drinking. I think we can draw on the passengers for this duty. It will be good for them to be active."

"*D'accord, mon colonel.*"

"Now another big problem that we simply must face is food," Fathi went on in an authoritative voice. "These passengers cannot stand many more days of starvation. Alpulu was only a stopgap, but it did give us the strength to carry on a little longer. Now that we are facing an unknown number of days virtually marooned here, we shall have to form hunting parties."

"*Oui, mon colonel.*"

"We must find out if there are any firearms on board for the hunters."

"*Naturellement, Monsieur colonel*. Zer ees zee flare gun wheech we carry for emergencies and zee gendarmes weez zee prisoners are carrying rifles. And assuredly, some of zee passengers are carrying pistols."

"Certainly, I myself have one," Fathi said.

I shook my head in consternation. These all seemed to be very desperate measures indeed. "Well, I must get myself to the hospital car and see how everyone is getting along." I stood up to go.

"You deed a wonderful job last night, Mademoiselle." Monsieur Morand smiled at me. "You undoubtedly saved zat man's life."

I wasn't so sure that his life was saved, but I said, "We all did that together, Monsieur." I left to find Pierre and ask him for tea to take to the patients.

The dining car had been completely restored from the night before. There, the Austrian men (now out of cigars) were back to playing cards. All traces of blood had been washed away, and, although it was still almost deserted and dingy, I could hardly believe that it had been the firelit scene of a nightmare that would stay with me for all the years to come.

One sleepy attendant was on duty, half lying across a table at the entrance. I touched his shoulder, and he raised his head. I asked him to send a tray through to the hospital car. He told me that Pierre was out on the work detail at the locomotive, but that he would bring it to me himself. I thanked him and made my way forward to gather my medical team for the morning rounds.

Madame Rostova was sitting with her ambassador husband in his single compartment, where she spent all her time when she wasn't working in the hospital car. All her days, that is, but not her nights. Gabriella was dozing in the next car forward and Ambassador Bretean, from Rumania, was already ahead of us, as was Karim. They smiled at us when we arrived. "Good morning, Jeanne," Karim said. "How do you feel?"

"Pretty well, all things considered. Have you noticed that the passengers have the doors open on the snow-free side all along this train?"

"Yes," he said, looking out that side from a window. "It's great, isn't it? The sun positively feels warm."

"Well, that's nice, I guess," I answered with a frown, "but I'm not so sure it's a good idea for those children to be playing outside. It can only mean more fevers. None of them are properly dressed."

"Oh, Jeanne, you do fuss too much. Let them have fun. It will keep their minds off their stomachs."

"I suppose you're right at that," I admitted, still doubtful. "I've always been a worrywart." We turned to work on the patients. "You know, Karim, isn't it strange that almost all of these patients are refugees bound for Israel?" I was giving some antibiotic to a little girl with a high fever.

"Oh, perhaps not so strange," Karim answered. "They probably have the least resistance from their many years of hardship. Then, too, they have all come from the second- and third-class local expresses now found along this line."

"Yes, I suppose that's true. Let's go and see our patient from last night." (Was I avoiding him?)

"I wondered when you were going to mention him," Karim said. "I thought he would be the first thing on your mind."

"It is funny, isn't it? I guess I don't have much hope that he will make it, and I'm afraid to look at his face."

"Now don't be a chump, old girl. He's fine."

"Are you sure?" I asked. A feeling of relief washed over me.

"Why do you always ask me that?" Karim answered. "Of course I'm sure."

Amazingly enough, it was true. The man had a rather gray look of pain and suffering, but his fever was gone. And the Demerol seemed to be keeping the worst of the pain under control. Gosh, I worried to myself, I hope there is enough to get us to Istanbul. "Well, Karim, you're right again. Thank God that here is another man with a strong constitution. Is he Turkish?"

"Yes, he is, poor chap," Karim said. "I haven't felt it was exactly the right time to ask him what he did to get himself into this mess." We talked while we rebandaged the stump of his arm.

"Well, have you asked him his name?"

"Yes, it's Omar."

"All right, Omar, you're doing just fine," I told him and patted him on the shoulder. He had been watching us as we worked — watching us with those dull eyes of his — but when I spoke to him, he looked up at me, and just a hint of a smile touched those eyes.

"*Inshallah!*" he said in a low voice. Karim and I exchanged glances.

"But, *inshallah* is Arabic," I said.

"Oh, *inshallah* is used by everyone in the Middle East," Karim answered. I nodded. It was a miracle that he was still alive. No red streaks went up his arm, and the antibiotics were keeping out infection. We had very few left. I looked at Omar and bit a cuticle on my finger. Yes, it really was a miracle!

Engrossed in these jobs and passing out our dwindling supplies, we noticed only that the daylight seemed less. The sun was quickly gone, and a sharp wind started up out of another threatening sky. The landscape took on a forbidding aspect, and it quickly became clear that we were building for another storm. Oh, dear God, please no, I prayed silently.

Suddenly there were screams. I looked up from bandaging the Rumanian's head wound. From the window across from the open door of the compartment, I could see a man running away from the train toward . . . toward . . . What was that? I thought. He was sinking deeply into the snow with every step, breaking through the crust, in his mad dash. Karim yelled, and at that moment it became clear. "Oh my God! It's the wolves!"

They were about one hundred and fifty yards from the train, circling something. There must have been about four or five of them, and they were growling, snarling, and snapping, closing in on . . . Dear God in heaven! "It's one of the children!" I yelled at Karim.

The little boy was crying and screaming in the center of that hellish circle of wolves. It all happened so fast. Men were running from all the cars. We heard a shot. "Don't shoot!" someone yelled. "You'll hit the child!"

"Where did those wolves come from?" Karim screamed, as he ran for a door. It was true: there had been no sign of them that morning. Even though the men struggled through the snow, the weight of their bodies slowed them. The small boy was huddled near a slender tree, and the wolves were closing in. Most of us were paralyzed by surprise and terror at their muzzles dripping red. The father fought to reach his son, screaming continuously. One of the wolves turned from his gory work to attack him. The man had a knife and used it to good avail. Another wolf struck out at him. He staggered against the tree and began to climb. He could only watch as the wolves tore his son apart. He let out piercing cries, seeing that he was helpless.

The would-be rescuers were mainly without weapons, and all had to return to the train. The wolves were ravenous. The boy was already dead and the men could not reach the father in the small tree. His eyes were staring out of his head; his face was ashen in the graying light; his hand covered with blood. Was the blood his own, or the wolves', or his son's?

The wind strengthened until it was like the howl of banshees, and snow fell. The wolves fixed in place. The man stayed in the tree. Time . . . how much time had passed? We had to do something! More shots were fired. They drove the wolves snarling back into the mountains. Men rushed out into the darkness to get the father. It seemed to take them forever to reach him.

He didn't move. "Why doesn't he move?" I said to nobody at all. Women around me were openly sobbing.

Several men climbed into the tree to drag him down. They carried him back to the train. He was still – too still. And then we realized that he was frozen, frozen to death.

CHAPTER 12

HORROR HAD FOLLOWED horror. We had even been betrayed by the sun. We were totally deserted and lost. The engine and the prison-luggage car were now completely buried, hidden under the freshly drifting snow. The valiant work of the engineer and the digging crew had been for nothing. Monsieur Morand and Fathi had been forced to abandon the idea of work crews during the blizzard, which shrouded the more than four hundred international travelers in a mortal white cocoon. It seemed nobody cared we were there, although logically we all knew this could not be true. Still, the barrenness of the land, the hostility of the elements, the savagery of the wolves, all gave us a feeling of utter futility.

At least we had managed to silence the screams of the pitiful young mother of the little boy, who had lost half her entire family. She was sleeping now, drugged by the herbal narcotic tea. Her two remaining children watched over her.

A terrible apathy set in. What could we do against the brutal elements? Nothing.

We, the lucky ones in the sleeping cars, retired to our bunks. Others, not so fortunate, lay on the floors – the freezing floors – too tired even to stand up any longer. Outside, the storm roared; we slept. I don't know if it was sleep or coma. I remember feeling a terrible desolation, but physically, nothing. My eyes were closed, but I saw the raging storm from behind my lids. The windows were the 'lids' of the train – closed, covered with ice, and blocked with a white death which must surely overtake us all.

How many hours this coma endured, I cannot tell. The *chef de cuisine* had given up trying to keep his miserable stove in the kitchen lighted: there was no wood. Therefore, there could be no more hot tea. We must have been very close to death by the next afternoon. The storm had abated only a little. The wind still cried through the corridors, and the candles flickered for the last time. There was complete darkness. The only sounds besides the wind were the soft clicking of rosaries and the murmuring of prayer; the steady clicking of Muslim prayer beads, and the chanting of prayer; and the whisper of the Hebrew prayers of the Jewish refugees. My mind, too, felt frozen. I could only repeat over and over the Bahá'í prayer, 'The Remover of Difficulties': *"Is there any Remover of difficulties save God? Say: Praised be God! He is God! All are His servants, and all abide by His bidding!"* I didn't count the prayers; I just repeated them for hours on end.

Suddenly, when it seemed that all hope was lost, and even the whispered prayers were stilled, there was a pounding from the outside. At first we paid no attention to it, thinking it was the storm. But the pounding continued, became more insistent.

We struggled back from our coma-like, hypnotized half-sleep and forced ourselves to take note of the intruding noise.

Monsieur Morand, with the help of two attendants, forced the frozen door open a crack. There, almost invisible in the swirling snow, was a man. Not one, but many! They yanked the door all the way open and pushed up and into the car. It was the Turkish army. We were rescued! The men had tied themselves together to keep from being lost in the blizzard. Could it really be? We hugged them. We laughed. We cried.

They had left their trucks on a road that was startlingly close to us — not more than one kilometer away — and had struck out into the storm to reach us quickly. They were all volunteers. To us, they were all heroes — God's own emissaries.

Without waiting for the storm to stop completely, they began to dig. They had brought tools and cans of kerosene to light fires and free the lines. The teams of diggers were changed frequently because of the freezing air, which cut into their straining lungs like fire. No one knew how far they would have to dig. Their first objective was to restart the locomotive and use it to help them move the wall of snow and ice. The soldiers were cheerful. They had eaten that day — that very day. And they had slept in their own beds the night before.

The *chef de cuisine* broke up one of the dining room chairs and fed it carefully into the kitchen stove. Soon there was tea again, very sweet this time, since he had used up the remaining sugar in it. That gave us back our strength.

The leader of the rescue mission, a General Turbankilyos (his name reflecting his Greek ancestry), was a giant of a man, with a full beard and thick black hair — even his big hands were covered with hair. His black eyes sparkled. He sat with Fathi and me during one of his breaks. His mustache and beard were coated with ice when he came in. Fathi passed him the cognac bottle.

"Tell us, when shall we reach Istanbul?" I asked.

"Patience, Miss Jeanne. It won't be too long now. Down the track, beyond the next grade, we have stationed a new engine. The tracks are virtually clear in front of that one. We have raised some tents to feed you when we reach that point. "

I yelped with joy. Fathi looked proud of his army. This was truly going to be a rescue.

"We've been trying to reach you since before the storm began, but the snow blinded our drivers. We had to clear the road as we went," our giant savior continued. "Three reporters froze to death in their car trying to reach you," he said blandly. "They carried brandy, you see, and took too much and fell asleep. They were less than two hundred meters from a village, but they couldn't see it. We found them this morning." His grin seemed inappropriate. "Another train, just one day ahead of yours, had to be evacuated. They were housed at a small village with, ah, somewhat inadequate food and shelter." I shuddered. "They have had to be hospitalized," he continued. "You will see their train at the food tents."

We learned that the few helicopters the Turkish army had were powerless to fly, and that the Red Cross had given us up the day before. These men really were heroes. Before long the general stood up, stamped his boots to clear them of any remaining snow, and headed out into the darkness again.

More quickly than I would have believed possible, the engine gave a great cough and awoke to life again. A wild cheer arose from the whole train. Within the hour, dim light glowed again in almost all the cars. Wisps of steam rose from the couplings between the carriages, and small fires burned around the wheels to free them from the ice. With a terrific grating, the locomotive pushed forward – only a few feet, true, but it moved. Another cheer encouraged the workers.

Slowly, painfully, the wall of ice and snow was pushed back. First, the snow scoop in front of the engine would ram a hole into it, then the diggers would clear a space and the train would move forward a few feet. Over and over they alternated, with a series of jolts, until with another cheer, this time from the soldiers outside, the enormous snowdrift had been cleared. The diggers climbed aboard, and, with still another combined cheer, we began to move slowly through the night. The triumphant whoop echoed through the hills. We had beaten the storm, the snow, and the ice. We had bested the elements bent upon our destruction. We moved at no more than five miles an hour, but we moved. And we were going downhill.

Another hour and the train ground to a halt. We all groaned, but Monsieur Morand was enthusiastic. "No, mademoiselle," he said. "Don't worry. We have arrived at zee food tents. We must all get down now."

A soldier appeared at Fathi's compartment to take over the vigil of his papers, and for the first time he was able to move around. Freedom at last!

The khaki-colored tents were huge affairs, with fires burning in front of them and the familiar potbellied stoves inside for warmth. Our group gathered around one of them. We had been through so much together; we automatically came together, like a family at a picnic. That was the atmosphere: fiesta time! Long tables lined the walls laden with caldrons of soup and mounds of the round (but not so hard) bread, for dipping. Faces were flushed, and teeth shone in grateful smiles. The night was dark, but inside the tents we were warm and safe.

"General," I asked, "did you bring a doctor with you?"

He looked somewhat crestfallen, but then brightened. "No, our doctor was in Istanbul when we left. But we have a medic."

"Wonderful!" I croaked. "Where is he? He will be able to help with the injured and ill."

"He's already with them, miss. He has a platoon working to feed them. Don't worry, they'll be all right."

"Come on, Karim," I tugged at his arm. "Let's go see how they're getting on."

We hurried back out into the night. Along a siding we saw the other train, the one that had been abandoned. It was filled with ice – its wheels and even the cars, including their contents, buried beneath the relentless white mass. There was no hospital car: somehow the barriers between people, which had fallen so easily in our train, had remained high here. How could the simple lesson of unity have been overlooked, especially in the face of such dreadful consequences?

One of the passengers of that tragic train had been frozen, and his dead body was found encrusted with ice. Karim took my hand. I shivered with nerves and cold.

The fires in front of the tents sent racing shadows across the narrow strip of packed snow between these shelters and the train.

When we reached our train, soldiers were still herding the passengers into the security of the canvas enclosures. Half-frozen and nearly hysterical with exhaustion, still the weary travelers were jubilant. Smiles were everywhere. Karim pulled me up into the hospital car. Even here the round, wood-burning stoves had appeared, and the cars were thawing out. The patients looked comfortable and cheerful. The young Turkish medic was supporting an old lady's head and tenderly spooning soup between her swollen lips. Karim went down the car to help with the feeding, and I was left to communicate by gestures with the medic. There was really nothing to say. I beamed at him and he beamed back. He pointed to our prisoner, Omar, with a questioning look in his eyes. I nodded and his look changed to a gratifying one of respect. There was nothing more for me to do here. Happily, I turned to leave.

Once more back outside the train, work crews were beginning the additional repairs we needed before we could continue on the last lap of our journey to Istanbul. General Turbankilyos had thought of everything. To entertain us and keep our minds from the persistent storm that howled outside our fragile shelters, he had brought a film. I couldn't believe it! There, in this desolation, far from civilization, after having been attacked by wolves, by starvation and Arctic-born blizzards – there we were, sitting in front of a movie screen. The film was in Turkish, and not many passengers could understand it. But we all sat captivated – hypnotized. I started to laugh hysterically. Fathi shook me – hard – and forced a glass of something terribly strong between my lips. I sputtered, coughed, and tears poured down my cheeks. Tenderly, he put his arm around me, and I cried into his rough overcoat – tears that, for once, didn't freeze to my cheeks.

CHAPTER
13

THAT NIGHT WE ALL really slept. The train moved slowly through the countryside. The clackety-clack of the wheels was a symphony.

It was very late morning when I awoke, and I looked out on a yellow countryside. Where was the snow? Eagerly, I came down from my berth and ran down the corridor to Fathi's compartment. He smiled.

"The snow is behind us in the mountains," he said. "We shall reach Istanbul this afternoon. It really is all over now."

I gathered my things together. The roofs of the city were coming into view. In the distance we could just see the cupola of one of the greatest churches in the world – the Basilica of St. Sophia. First built in 347 A.D. by Emperor Constantine, it was destroyed by fire, rebuilt, destroyed again in war, and rebuilt by Emperor Justinian – but was now dedicated to Islam. We could see the streets were cobbled. Lacy arabesques faced many buildings. There was the exterior of Topkapi and the domed roofs of the *Kapali Carsi* – the covered bazaar – a city in itself.

I sighed. It was like arriving in the midst of the Arabian Nights. Yet surely our adventure was behind us. I looked down at my swollen, cracked hands. They were still bleeding in spots – proof that the whole thing had not just been a bad dream. Fathi, Karim, and I had already exchanged addresses with insistent promises to keep in touch. I felt a soft sadness to think we probably would never meet again.

I thought back again over the journey, trying to make sense of it all. I had known great fear. I had dreaded being alone, though not once on the entire trip was I really alone. Rather, I was constantly surrounded by helpful hands and protection and care. I was still on my way to Haifa, but I felt that I had already made a pilgrimage – a pilgrimage to a pilgrimage, a consolation and a lesson, perhaps many lessons.

Slowly the train pulled into the station. I could see a long cafe backed onto the platform. In front of it were masses of people to greet us. Soldiers hanging onto the outside of our train were waving to Red Cross officials. There was the mayor, and the foreign service people, flanked by the U.S. consul. The French and British consuls began to wave. There were the local Bahá'ís: they must have been notified by the Austrian National Spiritual Assembly at Vienna. It was an

Official Welcome. There was cheering and music. The *Compagnie* was there, from the highest official to the lowest clerk. There were many reporters, and even television cameras in the background.

Cameras flashed as we alighted. Somebody from the foreign office came up and said that an airplane had been put at our disposal from Ankara for the rest of the journey to Israel. They asked me to go along. I said, no, I would continue from Istanbul by ship.

Just then, I was surrounded by the friends. They were all weeping. I was introduced to one distinguished Bahá'í gentleman, an Afnan, a relative of the Báb. He gathered me into his arms with tears streaming from his eyes, and said, "You have made this pilgrimage in the footsteps of Bahá'u'lláh, almost exactly one hundred years after His memorable journey from Constantinople to Adrianople! I have always wanted to do this, but I have never been permitted to do so. Now you have done it!"

"I don't understand," I said, utterly confused.

"You arrived at Edirne?"

"Yes," I answered ruefully. "And they stamped 'Edirne' right over my precious visa to the Cocos-Keeling Islands!"

"My dear, Edirne is the Turkish name for Adrianople," Mr. Afnan said quietly. "They stamped your visa with the name of the 'Land of Mystery!' What a blessing!"

A chill went down my spine. I remembered the

harrowing journey of Bahá'u'lláh in the winter of 1863 through the snow to Adrianople – the hardships, the hunger, the cold. I remembered that He had made that journey *by horse*.

My retracing of His steps to Constantinople – now Istanbul – had taken exactly nine days.

EPILOGUE

AN EARLY MORNING in Istanbul. The Turkish boat moved gently at the pier. A low mist shrouding the crowded harbor of the Bosporus lifted slowly, as a wintry sun raised its pale head from behind the immense dome of the Blue Mosque. A sleepy steward took my bags up the gangway. Faithful friends waved from the dock. The lines were taken in, and we began our slow advance through the strait to the Mediterranean.

The sea was choppy. I stayed in my berth. The ship moved closer to Haifa as I slept.

One morning we docked at Cyprus. There was fighting in the streets. The captain didn't want us to leave the ship. I appealed to him to permit me to go into town just long enough to place a call to mother in Connecticut. It had been impossible to call from Istanbul: I never found out exactly why. Reluctantly, he agreed.

There were tanks in the streets, and an occasional shot rang out to mark our passage through this revolution-marked island. The taxi waited for me at the telephone office. Almost immediately I heard mother's beautiful voice: "Darling! Where are you?"

"Cyprus, Mum. Have you received my letters?"

"No. Oh, darling, it is so good to hear your voice!" She began to cry.

"Don't cry, Mum. I've had the most remarkable journey. You'll never believe it!"

"Oh, yes I will. They called me from the travel agency. They had received word that you were dead!"

"What? But that's impossible. The train was in trouble, but we got through all right."

"I don't mean the train. That story has already been in the papers. I mean the plane."

"What plane?"

"The plane to Israel that crashed. It killed everybody on board."

Then I remembered. At the station, the foreign office man who offered to send me on the plane to Haifa. "Oh Mother, I told you that I would go by sea: it's the only way to see the Shrine of the Báb on Mount Carmel."

"That's what I said to the man from the travel agency — that you had promised me to go by ship. Oh darling, I am so grateful that you are all right."

"Now don't worry, Mum. Bahá'u'lláh is taking very good care of me. Goodbye now, I'll call you from

Haifa." Gently, I cradled the receiver on the hook. Yes, He had cared for me every step of the way. I thought of those poor souls on the plane. They had come through the ordeal of the train only to die on the plane. A mystery . . . an unsolved mystery.

Again, very early in the morning. The stars had faded into the pre-dawn light. We would reach Haifa this morning. Refugees from many countries crowded the bow of the ship – waiting, with me, to see the first glimpse of the Promised Land. Many were praying. Sometime during the night, we had passed the entrance to the prison-city of 'Akká – the Acre of the crusades – the fortress-city in which Bahá'u'lláh was imprisoned for so many years. My eyes filled with tears thinking of His suffering.

Just then, the tip of the sun pushed over the horizon and struck the dome of the Shrine of the Báb, nestled in the green heart of Mount Carmel. A ray of gold glistened in the sun. Soon the whole golden dome was haloed in light. My heart filled with praise of God and gratitude for His love and care. The world around me was filled with prayer and love. The end of a journey – the beginning of a new pilgrimage.

STAMFORD ADVOCATE, WEDNESDAY, FEBRUARY 13, 1963.

Weather-Caused Suffering Told In Letters Home

"I just do not know how it is possible for six or more international trains to be lost for nine days with hundreds of international passengers aboard and nobody investigates—not one word in the papers—it seems unbelievable that such a thing could happen in this century."

This is what Mrs. Jeanne Frankel of 444 Bedford St., wrote to her mother, Mrs. Margaret Bates of the same address in a recent letter, telling of her experience on a train from Bulgaria to Istanbul.

Mrs. Frankel, on a "once-in-a-lifetime" pilgrimage to the Bahai shrines on Mt. Carmel in Haifa, Israel, wrote of just a few of the never-to-be-forgotten experiences she had on a train that took nine days to make a trip that normally takes but two.

Painful Progress.

Because of the terrible snow and ice storms in Europe during January, the train was, at times, able to move only a few feet at a time.

In one tiny town, where there was a sugar factory, wrote Mrs. Frankel, more than

Writes Of Peril

MRS. JEANNE FRANKEL

100 people were evacuated from the train and housed in the village. But there was not enough food and many of the people had to be hospitalized.

Mrs. Frankel wrote to her mother by candlelight while still on the train, saying that they were without lights and had eaten nothing but coarse food. This was on Jan. 26 and the train had left for Istanbul on Jan. 21.

However, Mrs. Frankel stated that she was better off than hundreds of others who were crowded into the other cars. She had a small compartment, which she shared with an ambassador's wife.

"Everything is covered with snow, and it is still snowing," she wrote.

Well Stocked.

Mrs. Frankel was lucky because she had started the journey with a shopping bag full of food. As she boarded the train she wondered to herself why she had bought so much food. It turned out to be needed badly.

A practical nurse, Mrs. Frankel had a chance to put her medical knowledge to use before the journey was over. In one day, using her scant supply of aspirin and alcohol, she aided more than 400 persons, but could only offer a kind word to many who were suffering from flu, diarrhea, shock, exhaustion and starvation.

Act Of Kindness.

Her own hands were almost frozen and "a kind Bulgarian lady" when she thought Mrs. Frankel was sleeping, rubbed Mrs. Frankel's feet to keep them them from freezing.

All the details of the trip have not yet been told by Mrs. Frankel but she has promised to put them on tape and send them to her mother for, since she also writes and gives lectures, she is not expected to return to Stamford until June.

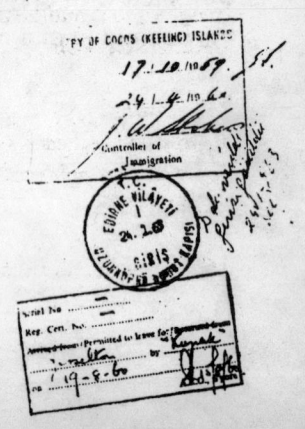

ONEWORLD
Books for Thoughtful People

MAIL ORDER

Drawings, Verse & Belief
Bernard Leach

Born in Hong Kong in 1887, Bernard Leach was a potter of world renown whose life and work bridged the traditions of East and West. This beautiful, cloth-bound gift edition combines the author-artist's delicate visual images and delightful verse with an impassioned profession of faith, to provide a rare insight into the personality of a great master craftsman.

"It is heartening, towards the end of our confused and fragmented century, to be reminded that wholeness is, after all, possible, and to be offered so beautiful and genuine an example of its achievement."
– RESURGENCE

"The anthology . . . provides a valuable commentary to the appreciation of Leach's poetry, and offers new insight into the mind of a man who embraced the most diverse cultures and art forms."
– CRAFTS

160pp cloth 82 illns £12.95/US$19.95

VALLEY OF SEARCH
A Personal Quest for Truth
Angela Anderson

Dissatisfied with the pampered, protected world of her childhood, Angela Anderson set out on a personal search for truth that took her through the spiritual and philosophical experience that was the late 50's and 60's. This is the story of that journey. Encounter Ouspensky, Gurdjieff, Alice Bailey, the early days at Coombe Springs, Pak Subuh, the Bahá'ís, and the followers of many other faiths. Sharing with readers all the joys, frustrations, hopes and - above all - the lessons of the journey of a lifetime, her down-to-earth, humorous and uplifting story will touch the hearts of all seekers.

192 pp softcover £6.95/US$11.95

ONE PEOPLE, ONE PLANET
The Adventures of a World Citizen
André Brugiroux

Dubbed the 'Marco Polo of Modern Times' André Brugiroux left France with 10 francs in his pocket to begin an epic eighteen-year journey round the world that was to take him some 250,000 miles to some of the remotest regions on earth.

From Indian Ashrams to war-torn Vietnam, from the materialistic fleshpots of California to the jungles of Borneo, Brugiroux survives it all with his good humour and irrepressible curiosity intact. More than just a 'rough guide' to the world, Brugiroux's adventures provide a true appreciation of the human race in all its diversity.

324 pages 12 photos softcover £7.95/US$13.95